THE PRACTICE

OF PEACE

5/31/05

Carey,

Hope you enjoy. For
me, the concepts and ideas
here have been worth
pondering + experimenting
with.
Looking forward to working
with you! With deep respect.
John

For more information or to purchase this or other publications, please contact:

Human Systems Dynamics Institute
50 East Golden Lake Road
Circle Pines, Minnesota 55014

Phone/Fax: 763.783.7206
Toll free: 866.473.4678
Or online at: www.hsdinstitute.org

ISBN 0-9740498-1-6

A Note on This Publication

The initial publication of this book was the result of a collaborative, worldwide effort undertaken by a remarkable community of people which has formed around the use and practice of Open Space Technology. The book was written by Harrison Owen, who remains solely responsible for the content—good, bad, or indifferent. Joelle Everette volunteered her time and skills for the tedious process of text editing, thereby correcting the multiple egregious errors of punctuation and spelling perpetrated by the author. Printing and distribution was accomplished by many people in multiple places: Germany/Michael M Pannwitz, United States/Peggy Holman, Canada/Larry Peterson, Australia/ Brian Bainbridge, Sweden/Thomas Herrmann, Haiti/John Engle, Taiwan/Gail West, Israel/Tova Averbuch. The efforts of this group were incredible, and in record time the book was made available around the world for those who cared to read it. For lack of a better designation we called it Global Chaordic Publication. At the time of publication it was noted that *The Practice of Peace* was a work in progress. That work has proceeded, and now with many thanks to the good people of Human Systems Dynamics Institute this second edition is available.

THE PRACTICE OF PEACE

TABLE OF CONTENTS

PREFACE

On September 11, 2001, our world changed yet again. Four airplanes took off for routine flights on a cloudless morning, filled with passengers expecting nothing more than a continuation of their lives as they had come to know them. There was business to be done, families to raise, friends to see.

Sitting among these passengers were a group of young men with very different expectations. They knew they were going to die, and had every hope that their deaths would right the terrible wrongs they perceived.

Within an hour of take off, all four flights ended in a fiery cataclysm that caused thousands more to die, and the whole world held its breath. For a moment out of time, millions of people, in every corner of the planet, found themselves locked in a common space as the television monitors displayed pictures of rising plumes of black smoke darkening the cloudless blue skies of New York City and Washington, D.C.

When breath returned, the commonality of the moment shattered. With the next breath many gave voice to anger, anguish and pain. And many others gave voice to shouts of victory and joy. The lethal divisions of our world became startlingly clear in an instant.

In truth, the world had not really changed. The hungry still needed food, and the well-to-do continued their diets. People made love, children were born, business was done, and the sun and the moon marked the passage of days as they had before that moment out of time. However, our perceptions had changed, and as usual, perception *is* reality. But what, exactly, is this new perception, and what reality has it created? I, along with everybody else, pondered these questions, not in some abstract, academic fashion, but with the raw existential tumult that occurs when all the pieces of your life are thrown in the air, and come down in massive confusion.

I had recently passed my 65th year, having known a rich, full life of shared experience with thousands of people around the planet. Villagers in West Africa, the dispossessed of American cities, sugar workers in Latin America, corporate executives in the US and Europe, government officials of all sorts, and just plain folks, all had contributed to the rich tapestry that my life became. If I had a driving passion, it was to think about, write about, and work with the phenomenon of transformation in our common lives. Along the way, I was privileged to stumble upon a funny way to hold meetings, which has traveled under the name of Open Space Technology. And suddenly that, too, was caught up in the whirlwind of the instant.

The details of my personal odyssey are of no consequence, but in January of 2002, I found myself in Israel, and more specifically on the rooftop terrace of a friend's apartment near Tel Aviv. I had come to that troubled part of the world to share whatever I could that might be of assistance. The news reports were filled with bombings and death, but the evening was silent and clear. A gentle breeze caressed my cheeks, and I found myself caught between the serenity of the moment and the hellish despair which pervaded the land. Somehow, in the open space between serenity and despair, words formed on my lips. "It is all about *The Practice of Peace*," I said to the night.

In the moment, as is usually true at such moments, clarity of insight was possible only because of the lack of details. Subsequently, details have emerged and pieces have begun to fit. In the pages that follow, I would like to share the results.

Harrison Owen
Camden, Maine
September 2002

FOREWORD

While scientists and mathematicians explored theories about why complex systems self-organize, Harrison Owen was setting conditions for people to experience self-organizing dynamics. Based on his own knowledge of human dynamics, an intuitive sense of the power of engagement, and a classical view of meaning-making in social systems, Owen developed a practice that makes the theory of complexity come to life for individuals and groups.

Thousands of people have used Owen's Open Space Technology to funnel their passion and responsibility into shared action. Hundreds of facilitators around the world use his simple and elegant method to open space for conversation that transforms chaos, confusion, and conflict into productive energy. Anyone who has participated in an Open Space event can attest to the incredible power of this simple self-organizing process. Though formal research on the method is skimpy, there is ample anecdotal evidence that Open Space Technology makes it possible for people to transcend traditional barriers to discover shared goals and to work together to accomplish them.

In *The Practice of Peace* Owen unfolds the foundations of his practice. He explores some of the theories that have informed him and begins to explain WHY the simple rules of Open Space Technology release powerful energy of human systems dynamics. We believe this is an important book in the evolution of the emerging field of human systems dynamics for three reasons.

First, the dynamics of human systems can be either unbelievably productive or massively destructive. The histories of humanity give ample examples of both extremes of self-organizing patterns. As our world grows smaller and our tools of destruction grow stronger, we must develop conscious competence about how our collective patterns form and how we as individuals and organizations can act responsibly in unpredictable and complex situations. Open Space is one way to increase our consciousness of emergent patterns, multiply our options for action, and help us shape our collective responses.

Second, as theoreticians and practitioners in this emerging field of human systems dynamics, we work in the tension between theory and practice. Many of us bring tools and insights into communities and organizations that teach us valuable lessons about setting conditions for productive self-organizing processes. As practitioners we need shared language and theory to generalize our findings beyond our local clients and their contexts. Other pioneers in the field focus on models and theories that build our understanding of complexity and its implications for human systems. As researchers we need pragmatic methods to test our emerging hypotheses. All of us know that the work cannot move forward without both theory and practice, but the traditional chasm between the two makes engagement difficult. Because Open Space Technology is an elegant and widely-used approach, it can support a dialogue between practitioners and theoreticians. In short, it may be able to open space for human systems dynamics so we can integrate and transcend our own chaos, confusion, and conflict.

Third, there is a world-wide network of people who use Open Space Technology and its lessons to support individuals and organizations in productive decision making and action. It was this self-organizing network that first published *The Practice of Peace* and made it available worldwide. We thank them for their courage and commitment and hope that this new edition will support the work of the current network and the extension of the network into new communities.

For these opportunities and for a lifetime of service and inspiration, we thank you, Harrison.

Glenda Eoyang, Ph.D.
Executive Director
Human Systems Dynamics Institute
February 2004

CHAPTER I
Peace and the Practice of Peace

Peace. It is a wonderful word in just about any language. And strangely, it seems to be most commonly used in that part of the world where there is no Peace, by whatever definition. In the Middle East, virtually all parties greet each other with "Peace." *Shalom* in Hebrew and *Salaam* in Arabic. At time of meeting and again at departure, both Jew and Muslim invoke Peace. And they are not alone in the practice. Christians know The Kiss of Peace, and politicians run on Platforms of Peace. And people everywhere have gone to war in search of Peace.

Obviously the word, and what it connotes, has great importance in our lives, but its meaning, at least in common usage, is more than a little elusive. It is possible to understand the universal Semitic practice as more in the nature of a hope or prayer than a confirmation of present reality, but the meaning of the word remains a will-of-the-wisp. Like the word "Love," the meaning of which stretches all the way from raw fornication up to and including "the essence of Divinity," so also "Peace" seems patient of a multitude of interpretations.

For many of us Peace is defined by the absence of its opposites, such as chaos, confusion and conflict. Absent any or all of these and we have Peace, and the way to Peace obviously would be the elimination of this unholy trinity. But what sort of Peace would we have? Unfortunately, I think the answer would be a state of affairs that is pretty boring. Peace under these terms would amount to some static, frozen, idealized circumstance. In the hot moments of living, we might look at such a state with envy, but as a long term reality, we may just have thrown the baby out with the bath water. In the name of preserving life, we would have removed precisely the elements that make life possible.

The temptation to desire a life devoid of chaos, confusion and conflict is quite understandable, if only because all three produce circumstances that are decidedly uncomfortable. Given any reasonable choice, who would want such a life? Unfortunately, I suspect all three come with the territory, and are not to be considered under the heading of unnecessary nuisances. For the truth of the matter is that chaos, confusion and conflict are integral to the process of living, and each brings its own special gifts, without which life, in the fullest sense of the word, is scarcely worth living. Heresy, some would say, but let us look more closely, starting with the "biggie," *Chaos.*

CHAOS

From ancient times to the modern day, Chaos has been scorned in polite society. And for good reason; Chaos makes a mess. Chaos comes in an infinite variety of sizes and packages, but all share a common trait: they do violence to the established order. Rather like a skunk at a garden party, or a bull in a china shop, when chaos raises its head, the old order stands in jeopardy.

Human beings, as indeed most critters in nature, become very attached to order, which provides the shape and structure of our lives, gives us meaning, and allows for the tidy planning of our futures. Should the agent of chaos be a rampaging river, our response is to raise the levies and protect our towns. Change "river" to "volcano" and the response is rather the same, but usually much less effective, for molten lava tends to run its own way. Contemporary corporations are no less adverse to the appearance of chaos, and when one implodes due to competitive pressures, change in consumer interests, or because of internal corruption and greed, the response is not unlike ants when their hills are under attack. At first they scatter and run, but soon they may be found attacking the invaders and rebuilding the ruins.

No news here. Chaos is not a welcome guest, now or ever. But it may be important to notice two responses to the chaos-laden situation for human beings: outrage and control. Indeed these two go together, for the basis of the outrage is often the loss of control. Somewhere along the line we humans developed the notion that we are supposed to be in charge, and when things go contrary to our expectations, we are not pleased. I grant that this idea seems to have some validity, if only because our dominant position is carefully written into some of our oldest and most revered sacred texts. For example, in the book of Genesis in the Old Testament (for Christians) or Torah (for Jews), it is decreed by God, no less, that we are to have dominion over the earth and all her creatures. We are definitely in charge, or so it might seem.

I leave the detailed exegesis of this text to the experts, but I would point out that this idea of being in charge has its limita-tions, not the least of which is that it never quite seems to happen. Despite our best efforts, rivers rampage, volcanoes explode, our businesses go kaput, and the ants invade our picnic. If we are supposed to be in charge, something is definitely wrong.

Part of what's "wrong," I think, is our inability to comprehend the enormous complexity of the cosmos in which we reside, albeit in a very small and insignificant corner. Being in control, or in charge, requires that you have some idea of what's actually happening, "get a number on it," so to speak. True we are gaining some knowledge, and perhaps even have a general idea of the forces at work and the elements at play. But it seems that the more we know, the more we discover our ignorance, and when it comes to turning knowledge into power, we are playing catch-up. After all we can't even accurately predict the weather on this silly little piece of solar driftwood we call home, let alone control it.

And then we come to the matter of outrage. Somehow it seems that the universe is not treating us correctly. When a river takes out a town, a hurricane batters the East Coast of the United States, a typhoon swamps a Pacific isle, or our business goes bump, something inside us demands that the Ruler of the Universe take counsel with us, for clearly there has to be a better way.

But it could be that the way the Universe has chosen has not done at all badly. After all, because of typhoons and hurricanes rock crumbles into fine sand, without which it would not be possible to have a nice day at the beach. And when our favorite business closes, typically a space in the competitive environment opens for new business and new ideas. It is painful for us to be sure, but not all that bad for the consumer and the world at large. There seems to be a rhythm here. You have to plow before you can sow and reap. Breathe out before breathing in.

Chaos appears in multiple forms. It is always painful if you happen to be caught in the path, but for all that pain there appears to be a purpose—opening space in the old order so that the new may appear. It might just be that this life we hold so dear is less about the established forms, and existing order, than the journey itself. In which case the chaos we experience is by no means just a painful incidental, but rather an essential component, for the journey would clearly cease without open space in which to move forward. And when it comes to our notion of Peace, I would suggest that Peace without chaos would be no Peace at all.

CONFUSION

Confusion is the intellectual equivalent of chaos. Just when you thought you had it all figured out, the path straight, the map set, suddenly the world changed, and somehow it did not match what you were planning on. It was a surprise, and definitely not a nice one, particularly for those of us who take pride in our rational capacities, our ability to look the future dead in the eye and come up with a winning plan.

Plan-makers everywhere fall prey. The general whose carefully crafted battle plan gets lost in the mists of war. The CEO, whose business plan looked great on paper and in all the "PowerPoint" presentations, suddenly discovers that the yen has fallen through the basement when "The Plan" was directed towards the Japanese market. And the dissolution of nice plans is not an experience limited only to business folks and generals. Lovers have the same dilemma. That great life plan which included graduate school, building a career, creating a little capital for investment, all go out the window when that special she or he appears and whisks you off to Bali. In all cases, it's confusion.

The consequences of confusion can be painful, but the major pain, I think, is to the ego. We really thought we had it pegged, but we didn't. Our problem, it turns out, is that we had forgotten Korzybski's[1] famous dictum, "The map is not the territory." To be sure, maps are useful, but never to be confused with the land they depict, just as menus are not the meal, nor is the book the experience.

---

[1] Korzybski, Alfred, *Science and Sanity* (Fifth Edition) Institute of General Semantics, 1994.

The cloud of confusion, however, holds a silver lining. For as the faulty maps of our fertile minds are dissolved in the acids of life experience, we find the page wiped clean so that we can begin again. If we are wise, we will remember the lessons of our confusion, even as the good general recognizes that the battle plan goes out the window when the first bullet is fired. The activity of planning is still a valid one. Its validity, however, does not come from the plan's capacity to create the future, for the future almost inevitably has a mind of its own. But the plan is a great place to start, and a wonderful checklist of things to notice along the way.

In a word, confusion clears the mind of all we thought we knew, or suspected, so that we can truly appreciate what actually transpires. Without confusion we would be condemned to live in a world of old maps and outdated plans which quickly become dogmatic pronouncements. And the dead weight of dogma is something a vital mind can live without. If wisdom begins with an acknowledgment of our limitations, confusion may be an essential first step.

CONFLICT

If ever there were a true opposite of Peace, conflict would appear to be it. Even conflict, however, has its positive side. The presence of conflict in the human community means quite simply that people care. Show me any organization or situation where there is no conflict, and I will show you one where nobody cares. And without caring, without some real passion, the long term vitality of that organization is in jeopardy. Conflict only becomes a problem when people run out of space.

The appearance of conflict in our lives indicates hot points of growth. In the realm of ideas, philosophies and paradigms, to which might also be added social systems and technologies, conflict not only indicates points of growth, but is also essential for the growth process.

Thomas Kuhn, in his seminal work, *The Structures of Scientific Revolutions,*[2] describes the progress of science in terms that many have found uncomfortable. In the place of the nice, neat, linear, rational rolling out of scientific discovery described in many high school and college classrooms, he relates a tale filled with explosive jumps and massive conflicts which not only characterize the process, but are seemingly essential to its progress. As paradigm succeeds paradigm the process is characterized by discomfort at the beginning (things just don't seem to fit anymore, and confusion abounds) and culminating, more often than not, in massive confrontation, as an older view of the established order gives way to a newer, and usually more adequate, one. Along the way, the presence of conflict gives rise to a clarification of vision as differences are perceived, formulations rationalized and new data considered. At the end, a new paradigm emerges, a new map of our world. And then the process begins again, for it remains true that the map is not the territory.

The world of scientific inquiry may seem abstract, and far removed, from the everyday world of our common experience, particularly as we witness the bloody consequence of conflict in the hot spots of The Middle East and elsewhere. But it is probably worthwhile noting that even in the temple of science things can become very heated, and sometimes result

---

[2] Kuhn, Thomas, *The Structures of Scientific Revolutions,* University of Chicago Press, 1962.

in disastrous consequences, as Galileo discovered in his struggles to articulate his new map of the cosmos. It would be very nice, of course, if disastrous consequences could be avoided, but not through sacrificing conflict through which ideas are sharpened and clear positions formed. It turns out that physicists and astronomers are passionate, too. They care deeply about what they do. Absent the passion, and we would probably still be living on a flat earth. When two passions collide there you have conflict, but you also have the intellectual heat and desire that transmutes half-formed ideas, clouded in confusion, into blinding new insights. The problem, I suggest, is not the conflict, but rather that there is insufficient space to work things out. Destructive conflict occurs when you run out of room—physically, emotionally, intellectually, spiritually. Thus, the answer would seem to be: open more space.

The applicability of Kuhn's insights to the broader world of human affairs is amply demonstrated by the rapidity with which his notion of paradigm, and paradigm shift, have found a place in the thinking and vocabularies of those in business, government, non-profits, and the whole broad range of human institutions. As a testimony to the pervasive impact of his thinking, it appears that many folks have forgotten (if they ever knew) that it was Thomas Kuhn who started the whole thing rolling. No discussion of organizational change seems to move very far without the magic word *paradigm* putting in an appearance. It is interesting to notice, however, what is typically *not* a part of such discussions: conflict and its potential benefits.

As Kuhn's thinking has moved into the public domain, it has seemingly become domesticated and sanitized. Shifting paradigms becomes a matter of rational choice, or executive dictate, as in "We will have new paradigm thinking." Or, "Our business will operate according to the new paradigm." Doubtless there are elements of rational choice and decision making in the shifting of paradigms, but that, I think, is just the tip of the iceberg. In truth, people care deeply, and have great passion for their old paradigms. No matter how attractive a new paradigm may sound, at the end of the day, it is not familiar, comfortable or secure. The passage from old to new will only be negotiated with chaos, confusion and conflict. It all comes with the territory, no matter how many consultants offer Programs for Painless Paradigm Progress. And there is even a more bitter pill to swallow. There is an end to the old paradigm. It dies. In rather dry tones, Kuhn says as much.

"But if new theories are called forth to resolve anomalies in the relation of an existing theory to nature, then the successful new theory must somewhere permit predictions that are different from those derived from its predecessor. *That difference could not occur if the two were logically compatible. In the process of being assimilated, the second must displace the first. (Italics mine)* "[3]

The ending of anything, be it a theory, a paradigm, a way of life, or life itself does not take place without trauma, and even on a good day, trauma is not something that most people look forward to. And yet the old dictum holds true: *In life only death and taxes are inevitable.* Actually, taxes may be avoided, which leaves death as the inevitability of life.

---

[3]   Kuhn, Thomas, *op cit* pg 97.

Peace and War

It is customary and understandable to juxtapose Peace and war. Presumably, when Peace is present, there is no war And yet if we are correct in the understanding that Peace must include and transcend conflict, along with chaos and confusion, surely it must also include and transcend war, which is an extreme expression of conflict.

It is, of course, entirely possible that the inclusion of war within an understanding of Peace is nothing more than an unfortunate consequence of my logic. It might be argued that war is so totally horrible that even though conflict may have a place in our understanding of Peace, war is something else. And yet I believe it fair to say that conflict appears in multiple forms ranging from mild to extreme, and although the intensity of conflict may vary, the essential effects are the same. Conflict in all of its forms, at every level of intensity, is an essential mechanism in the evolution of life of the cosmos and for our little part of life called *Homo sapiens.* If so, we are then confronted with the pointed and painful question: What good is war?

Nobody in their right mind would choose war, the bloody annihilation of opposing forces and innocent lives, until or unless all other possibilities had been exhausted. Yet there come times when such a choice appears inescapable. The young American colonies reached such a moment in their struggle with the British Empire. And many other people in different times and places have found themselves in similar positions. In the late 1930's the United States reached such a point again relative to the Axis powers. To be sure, there have been (and are still) sociopaths who live by war for their own personal gains and gratification, but that does not, I think, obviate the fact that life presents moments of choosing between fundamental core values and their dismissal. In the moment we are called upon to affirm that which we hold to be the good, true and beautiful, even at the cost of extreme sacrifice, or to walk away.

The pacifist would see all of this quite differently, or maybe use the same logic and come to a different conclusion. If human life is truly precious—even the lives of fascist dictators and perverted sociopaths—then no life can be taken. I respect and honor this position but cannot make it my own. There are many arguments pro and con, but none in my view are decisive. You simply have to make a choice, and it is always a tragic choice. For me there come times when war is inevitable, and in such a time I choose to engage the conflict to the best of my ability. Others can and will make a different choice, which brings me back to the original pointed and painful question: What good is war?

From where I sit, war, along with all the other cataclysms of life create the defining moments in which an old order is destroyed, and space is opened for new possibilities to emerge. Along the way we as humans often experience an outburst of technological advance driven by the adrenal rush of high conflict. Some of these technologies are purely destructive, but many find a positive place in our lives when the conflict subsides. From World War II we experience the gifts and terrors of the atom and radar/microwave as both destroyers and healers.

On a deeper level, war has provided the crucible in which our souls are tried. At one and the same time we perceive both the nadir and epitome of human behavior and it is not incidental that many of our great heroes and heroines have been made manifest in the fires of war. These are the people whose courage and compassion set new standards for our common behavior. War is also the special time for the Warrior and the Warrior Spirit.

The Warrior and Warrior Spirit

For many who pursue the cause of Peace, the Warrior stands as anathema, the antithesis of all that is peaceful. The Warrior is perceived simply as a brutal thug. I believe this to be a profound error. Doubtless there are brutes and thugs, but they are not true Warriors.

Native American tradition, along with many others, holds the Warrior in deep respect. Nowhere does this become more apparent than in the tradition of the Medicine Wheel.[4] The Medicine Wheel is simple in concept, albeit with many complex mutations. The essential statement is that all effective groups (families, clans, organizations, nations) have four elemental roles or powers: The Warrior, The Visionary, The Healer, and The Teacher. These four are represented by the four points of the compass, hence a wheel, as in Medicine Wheel. To the North is the Warrior whose power is manifest in explosive leadership, breaking through the old in order to open space for new being and possibilities. Without the spirit of the Warrior, a people would be stuck in the past, or simply disappear. But the presence of the Warrior is not without cost. In contemporary jargon this is called "collateral damage." And so to the South we find the Healer, the spirit of compassion which repairs the wounds occasioned by the Warrior's thrust towards future possibility.

---

[4] For a wonderful and powerful introduction to these traditions read *The Four-Fold Way* by Angeles Arrien (Harper/San Francisco, 1993).

The balm of healing too comes with a cost—it can be too comfortable, thereby deadening the restless spirit of a people. And so from the East comes the Visionary, whose clear sight sees beyond the explosive, painful moment of the Warrior, and the comforting balm of the Healer to the deeper possibilities inherent in whatever new reality may have been encountered. Here again, there is a cost, for while the Visionary perceives possibilities as yet unrealized, these possibilities will remain in the ethereal realm until anchored in the practicality of everyday life. And so we move to the West and The Teacher whose role is to communicate the lessons of life drawn from the fire of the Warrior, the balm of the Healer, and the insight of the Visionary. And yet these lessons also come with a cost. It is all too possible that the people will become stuck in the way things are and have been, weighed down by the heavy load of tradition. Once again it is the time for the Warrior to break the bounds and open space for new possibilities.

The simple, elegant Medicine Wheel makes it apparent that while each role is essential, none is sufficient by itself, for all roles bring their gifts, and all have their costs. Life becomes effective and powerful for a people with the presence and passage of The Warrior, The Healer, The Visionary, and The Teacher. But it all begins with Warrior.

Peace and the Warrior
I have suggested that conflict, even in its most extreme forms (war) must be included and transcended in our understanding of Peace. Strange as it may seem, Peace and War do not stand in opposition, but War, as all other manifestations of conflict, brings essential gifts to the progress of humanity, albeit very painful ones. And by extension, the Warrior also brings gifts which are essential, but not sufficient in and of themselves.

All of which raises an interesting question: Can the Warrior know Peace? Is it possible for the Warrior to be peaceful, not in denial of his or her essential character, but in fulfillment of it? Is the notion of a peaceful Warrior an oxymoron or a profound insight?

View from the Bhagavad-Gita

One of the oldest and most revered sacred texts in the world is The Bhagavadgita.[5] It is the story of enlightenment, or more exactly the means for enlightenment. Most remarkably, the central character is not an esoteric mystic, but rather a warrior prince, and the setting in not some reclusive cave, but a battle field prior to, and during, a major engagement. Perhaps most disturbing (or enlightening, depending upon your point of view) is the fact that as enlightenment proceeds and full self-awareness grows, the warrior prince does not become less a warrior, but rather more so. In a word, the hero, Arjuna, becomes fully and completely what he essentially is, a warrior prince. And in that moment, he becomes fully whole, healthy and harmonious with himself and with his environment. One might say he was at Peace, and the result was a battle won, and thousands died in that battle.

For those who might view any warlike, violent act to be the antithesis of Peace, and the Warrior to be Peace's major enemy, The "Gita," as the book is often referred to, stands as a major problem. Some would simply dismiss it, others interpret the battle as "spiritual warfare" where nobody really dies. I must leave this discussion to the competent scholars, but for myself, I find it hard to dismiss the "Gita" if only

---

[5] There are multiple versions of *The Bhagavad-Gita,* but the most accessible in my judgment for an English speaker is one done by an American friend, Jack Hawley. It was published by New World Library in 2001.

because it has been central to the life and practice of billions of people for thousands of years. Which of course does not make it "true," but certainly worthy of consideration? As for transmuting the battle into some ephemeral bloodless encounter, for me that is to rip the heart and soul from the tale. I am left with some definite conclusions.

First, conflict in all of its forms is an essential, albeit painful, element of life, and life without conflict is only a lobotomized shadow of its former self. Secondly, The Warrior, and the Warrior Spirit in each of us, is a central character in all of life—indeed it may well be the primary engine of life, that power which opens space (sometimes violently) so that life may be full. Always essential, but never sufficient, requiring the constant balancing presence of The Healer, The Visionary, and The Teacher. In a word, conflict must be included and transcended for life to be vital and Peace to reign. And a Practice of Peace which does not effectively deal with these realities is, at best, naive.

PEACE

How shall we understand Peace in ways that allow the inclusion and transcendence of the harsher realities of our lives? Peace without chaos, confusion and conflict is no Peace, not because we would not prefer it that way, but because each member of this unholy trinity makes a positive contribution to the process of living. Equally, Peace without ending and death is productive of an idealized, static life, stuck in its ways, precluding the possibility of any sort of evolution.

Had the Ruler of the Universe taken our council at the start, perhaps we could have suggested a better way. Indeed it seems that He or She almost had it right in those halcyon days of The

Garden of Eden (or whatever primal/primitive vision of our initial utopia). But then something happened. Some folks will see the departure from that happy place as the beginning of the end, and the source of all our problems. Personally, I see it as the end of the beginning, the starting place of an incredible human journey. In a word, we were kicked out of the nest and forced to fly. Like young eagles, we have been screaming ever since, and certainly our initial wing beats were frantic, verging on comical. But we have learned. Not without a multitude of rough landings and ill advised take-offs, to say nothing of more than a few "crash and burns." But we now know something of the joys of flight. For those who desire a return to that idyllic state, I say "lots of luck." And when the going genuinely gets tough in this thing we call life, I can certainly see their point. But at the end of the day, and indeed on most days, I choose to celebrate the rich heritage of *Homo sapiens,* crash landings and all. The flight of the human spirit is, for me, truly awesome. But you do have to leave the nest, and that departure has its consequences.

As for Peace, I like the metaphor of flying, all of flying, including first flights, last flights and bumps along the way. Peace then is a process, not a thing; a journey and not a destination. It is flow and not a state. *Peace is the dynamic interrelationship of complex forces (including chaos, conflict and confusion) productive of wholeness, health and harmony. The Practice of Peace is the intentional creation of the requisite conditions under which Peace may occur.* Peace, as far as I am concerned, is infinitely more than the cessation of hostilities, which often takes the form of bombing the offending parties into submission until they can no longer fight back. And Peacemaking neither starts nor ends at the negotiating table, for the objective is not just a set of treaty terms acceptable to all parties, but rather the renewal of meaningful and productive life for the planet, the nation, businesses, social institutions, the family, and each one of us.

Please do not expect a radical, new approach. In fact, I believe each and every one of us already has both the knowledge and skills necessary, and the fundamental mechanisms are essentially "hardwired" into our being. We have only to remember what we know, and practice what we are. I concede that the apparent simplicity of these affirmations verges on the naive. It may also be true that a blinding flash of the obvious may be good for the soul.

The core mechanism referred to above is self-organization, and a core practice is what we now call Open Space Technology. I will suggest that self-organization drives towards Peace and, when freely operative, is generative of the dynamic interrelationship of complex forces productive of wholeness, health and harmony. Open Space Technology (OST) is an extraordinarily simple approach which enables groups of people, large and small, to engage complex, chaotic, confusing and conflicted issues in a Peaceful fashion. Further descriptions of the approach and its various applications are presented in the following material and for a complete account, please consult my book, *Open Space Technology.*[6]

First utilized in 1985, Open Space Technology has now been applied thousands of times, all over the world, with virtually every imaginable sort of group. It's effectiveness as a tool for meetings is a matter of record, but many continue to find it strange, if not shocking. The reason is not hard to ascertain, for Open Space apparently violates essentially all theory and

---

6   *Open Space Technology: A User's Guide,* Berrett-Koehler, 1997.

practice of group organization. The notion that large groups of conflicted people could virtually instantaneously organize their affairs and pursue their tasks without elaborate pre-planning and a host of facilitators flies in the face of what appears to be the accepted wisdom. And yet the global experience demonstrates that every time a group of people gathers of their own free will, around an issue of strong common concern, the experience is repeated—provided they sit in a circle, create a bulletin board on which to identify issues, open a market place to arrange time and place particulars. Then they are on their way, typically in something more than an hour. From the point of view of what I might call "standard" theory and practice, what happens not only should not happen, but should not be possible. But it does happen. When viewed from what we are now learning about the power and function of self-organizing systems, the unbelievable becomes the predictable.

In truth, I find the Open Space experience much more interesting as an ongoing natural experiment in which we can both experience the reality of self-organization and learn to support and enhance that experience. The phenomenon of self-organization is a relatively recent discovery, and not an altogether comfortable one for those who have understood that order in our lives can only be the product of humongous effort. Recently, we have been learning that, given certain very simple preconditions, order just happens. We will be taking a look at some of these new learnings in Chapter IV.

From where I sit, Open Space does not contribute anything new, but rather helps us to see what is already a naturally occurring phenomenon. But just because it occurs naturally does not mean that we can't learn to use it, and learn to use it well, even as the natural occurrence of gravity can be used to our advantage. To the extent that self-organization in general, and Open Space Technology in particular, is productive of Peace, this is an experiment we must run. I hope that you will take everything I have to say as a testable hypothesis, which of course is a critical part of any experiment. Don't believe a thing, and certainly not on my say so. Do it, and if the experimental results are replicated, do it again and do it better. It could just be that Peace will break out.

TWO STORIES TO SET THE STAGE

In the early 1990s, I happened to be in South Africa a few weeks after Nelson Mandela was released from prison. For the vast majority of the population this release was an occasion for celebration and joy, others were not so sure, and everybody felt the deep anxiety characteristic of the onset of massive social change. With the approaching end of Apartheid, a dark period of the human story was seemingly coming to a close, but how it was going to play out remained a total mystery. Some saw only bloodshed and disaster. Others envisioned the dawning of a new golden age. For all of the uncertainty, one thing was clear: people needed to talk to each other, quickly and very deeply.

In Capetown, where I happened to be, a tense situation was made all the more so by virtue of the fact that Mandela's island prison lay just off the coast. My hostess, Valerie Morris, and her associates managed a hotel, and when they had sensed the moment, they immediately volunteered their facility as the site of potential conversation. Who, what and how remained to be determined.

Their decision was made on a Sunday, and by the following Wednesday a hundred or so people had agreed to show up several days later. It was quite a group ranging from the mayor of Capetown to young residents from the local township (Black area), with others coming from all over the local society including the ANC and Afrikaners. They all shared a common concern for their country, but most did not know each other, and certainly had had little occasion for any kind of conversation up to that present moment.

We met in Open Space. One hundred people sitting in a circle were invited to identify their passions and concerns for the future, announce them on sheets of paper, and take personal responsibility for their discussion. Within 20 minutes from start, multiple issues were posted on the wall, and one hour later discussions were under way. The issues were not the easy ones. Land reform, reparations, education, housing, employment—all made a showing. But the last one posted said it all. A young man from the township said, "I have one issue. Fear. My fear and our fear. And how do we get through it all."

From there it started. For 8 hours the discussion groups ebbed and flowed. Sometimes in anger, sometimes in silence, and occasionally with laughter. By the end of the day, we stood silently in a circle and then shared with each other what the experience had meant. There was anger, fear, hope, despair, and at the end silence, broken by a single voice saying, "I think we are the new South Africa, and we have a lot of work to do."

Final Peace did not arrive that day in Capetown. But in a very powerful sense, Peace was already there. Amidst the chaos, confusion and conflict, there was also a sense of connectedness, and people sang the songs of their homeland in the tongues of their birth. It is noteworthy that the whole enterprise was created in four days. There was one facilitator who spoke only briefly at the beginning, and never intervened in any way with any of the groups. The people did it all by themselves.

A Different Tale: USWEST

From a very different world, and slightly later in time (mid '90s) comes this story of USWEST (now known as Quest), an American phone company which found itself in some degree of difficulty. The sources of its difficulties were multiple, including the fact that a massive "Process Re-engineering" project had failed to take into account a major shift in their market. After several years of effort, costing many millions of dollars and involving massive amounts of executive time, the new organizational design was revealed. Unfortunately, there had been an unforeseen event in the form of major earthquakes in California. This caused many nervous Californians to seek other homes in such places as Washington State, Oregon, and the American Southwest—all of which were part of the area USWEST served.

The net effect was that projections for customer growth were off by wide margins, and the demand upon the system was almost more than it could tolerate. Installations of new phone lines, even emergency ones, could take as long as six months. Added into the muddle was the fact that a major part of the "re-design" included a substantial reduction of the work force, downsizing, as it was known. The net effect was a most unhappy situation, made even worse in the State of Arizona by the occurrence of a major flood. As most people know, floods are not supposed to happen in the desert, and when they do, the damage can be severe, particularly if you happen to be a phone company.

For the 5000 employees of USWEST in Arizona, "unhappy" was too mild a term. Angry, frustrated and confused, the employee's union let it be known that unless there were some serious conversations with management, prior to the beginning of contract talks, it was their stated intention to "have the company for lunch," as one Union representative explained it to me. The union suggested Open Space as the means.

Barely 6 weeks after the union's suggestion, 160 representative of the company, including the full management team and people from all the skills, trades and geographical areas in the company found themselves sitting in a circle at 9 a.m. There had been no warm-up, no training, no agenda building, no caucuses. There was only a focusing issue, stated as "How do we fix Arizona?" And nobody had any question that it was broke. There were obvious questions, however, as to whether anybody could be civil enough, or even wanted to be civil enough, to work together for a resolution. Looking at the surrounding faces, it was apparent that most people could not figure out whether they were attending a funeral for the company or the opening rounds of civil war. Peaceful it was not.

Following a brief 15 minute introduction, the assembled body answered the invitation to identify the issues and opportunities for fixing Arizona with a curious enthusiasm. Within 45 minutes, 60–70 issues had been posted on a large blank wall, people had signed up to participate in the multiple discussions, and it was off to work.

The first day was intense. Discussion raged, people came and went, and as one participant said, there was an incredible amount of anger and bitching. But it all held together, and on the second day the same participant said, "I think we are finding solutions for what we were crying about yesterday."

By the morning of the third day, it was quite a different world. Issues were prioritized, actions identified, and people accepted responsibility for carrying them out. But that was just the business side of things. Perhaps more significant was the atmosphere of the final gathering. One more time 160 people sat in a circle, but this time they were thanking each other for the opportunity to work together, and for the steps that were being taken. A final participant rose to address the group, a large union guy with tears running down his cheeks. He said something like, "As some of you know, I have had some trouble with my family. But I just want you all to know that I have found my family, and it is you."

When a group traverses the treacherous ground from incipient civil war to addressing each other as members of a family, it is clear that a profound shift has taken place. It was also clear that massive amounts of chaos, confusion and conflict remained to be dealt with, but the assembled folks had demonstrated, most importantly to themselves, that they were up for the task. Indeed, they had already been doing it. And they did it essentially all by themselves.

A STARTING POINT

It might appear from the two stories told above that Open Space Technology represents the magic bullet for Peace. That would be a profound error. It is only a start. The true power lies with the incredible capacity of self-organizing systems to create Peace for themselves and with their environment. Not all the time, not always perfectly, and not without continuing problems, but Peace, nonetheless. This power is owned by no one, and is available to everyone. We have only to use it.

Unpacking all of this, and making it practical is our task for the balance of this book. There is little need for yet another theoretical discourse on the nature of Peace, even less for impassioned exhortation. Theory is useful, and the temptation for exhortation understandable, but given the state of our world, practical application is essential. The manifestation of Peace in our personal lives, with our neighbors on this shrinking planet, and with the planet itself, is the first order of business, indeed it may be the only business—unless, of course, we choose to go out of business.

CHAPTER II
Piecemeal Approach to Peace

One needs scarcely more than a quick glance at the morning newspaper to see that there is indeed trouble in River City, to say nothing of Planet Earth. Leaving aside the normal, and usually productive, doses of chaos, confusion and conflict, it is apparent that the forces at play go much deeper. The overt manifestations of the pathology in our midst come in multiple forms, all of which might be summarized by two generalities: Organizational Dysfunction and Soul Pollution.

Organizational dysfunction is a bland short hand for the apparent fact that many, perhaps most, of our organizations and institutions are no longer capable of doing what they were designed to do. Nation states flounder as they seek to address the internal issues of their citizens, while simultaneously facing challenges posed by their neighbors in other nations, to say nothing of the deteriorating conditions of our natural environment. We have a new term—a Failed State, a condition which seems pandemic in Africa and the Middle East, epidemic in Latin America, and showing first symptoms in the Far East. Only the United States and Europe seem in marginally good health, and we aren't too sure about them.

The litany of disturbance and dissolution by no means stops with the largest of our institutions. Corporations and small businesses, city governments and town halls, social service organizations and philanthropic foundations, and last but not least, that smallest of organizations, the family, all seem to be in an increasing state of disrepair. Assembling and validating the necessary data to prove these assertions would be a monumental task with little to be gained, for although it is doubtless true that some organizations are doing better than others, it is quite clear that a significant number of people *think* something is profoundly wrong. And in this case, I would argue that perception is reality.

Just to make matters worse, the personal cost for each one of us individually is going up exponentially. I call it Soul Pollution. Early indications appear in our vague malaise when we face a new day. Not necessarily bad, but certainly not what we could call great. The source of our discomfort is unclear, and usually ascribed to the great, amorphous *they*. They did that, they did this, but truthfully nobody ever saw *they*. Whatever else might be happening, not too much of it relates to that soaring feeling when our spirits just fly. The old lament, "How can I soar with eagles when I have to live with such turkeys?" seems more appropriate. The terminal stages of Soul Pollution show up with the arrival of paralyzing stress and the abuse of almost anything, including substances, spouses and fellow workers. Not a happy situation.

THE "FIXES"

As each new set of problems appears, new fixes are created. For economic downturn we create stimulus packages, and when it appears that behind the downturn lies an uneducated work force, we initiate education development programs. Should it turn out that the workers can't learn because they are hungry or diseased, the fix is determined to be nutrition and health programs. Each of these several programs was well intentioned at the start—and possibly quite effective in terms of their primary objectives—but as they proceeded the unintended consequences were often more disturbing than the initial problems.

The strategy employed is an ancient and honorable one. Consider the area of discord, identify the constituent problems, break them down into manageable units (typically small), and create fixes appropriate to the problem. There is an obvious logic, even elegance to the approach, which we might call *Peacemaking in pieces.* Or less elegantly, eat the elephant one bite at a time. Unfortunately life turned out to be more complicated and interrelated than we thought, but that didn't stop us from trying over and over again.

In the middle '60s as Peace Corps staff in Liberia, West Africa, I and many others became aware of a real problem. Liberian children showed the unmistakable signs of malnourishment (swollen bellies and red hair), for which the cure appeared to be more food. And so, thanks to the infusion of American and international aid, large amounts of rice were imported and distributed. The children seemed to do somewhat better, but the imported (subsidized) rice had the unintended effect of lowering the price of rice in the market place and thereby making the local rice product non-competitive. This of course had a disastrous impact on the pocket books of the local farmers. But all was not lost. It seemed that the local farmers depended largely on so called "Upland Rice," which was planted on the hillsides. Upland rice is very tasty, but compared to Swamp Rice, very unproductive by a factor of 3–4. The solution was glaringly obvious: plant Swamp Rice. And because parts of Liberia receive something like 200 inches of rain each year, major portions of that country are essentially one big swamp. And so, at large expense, the Swamp Rice Project was begun.

After almost 10 years, the demonstration plots looked as beautiful as always, and their productivity was as anticipated, 3–4 times that of Upland Rice. However, the rate of adoption (old style farmers switching to new style rice) remained basically zero. What happened?

A small group of anthropologists took the bold step of talking to the farmers. It turned out that the local folks were well aware of the increases in productivity possible with Swamp Rice, however the mythology and lore of the area held that swamps were the home of some very nasty spirits, and who would want to go there? The swamps were also home to a beastly bug which causes Schistosomiasis, a terribly unpleasant and lethal disease. Adding insult to injury, the whole village life cycle was keyed to the cultivation of Upland Rice which extended over the course of a year. Festivals and celebrations took place as the annual cycle of preparation of the fields, planting, cultivation and harvesting occurred. Swamp Rice, on the other hand had three, possibly four crops a year, which threw everything out of kilter.

The net effect of massive effort and funding was that nothing changed, or more accurately, a lot of things did change, making the situation in many ways worse than it was to begin with. Say what you will about the village agricultural system based on Upland Rice, it worked, and had done so for millennia. For sure there were problems and shortages, but Upland Rice had one major advantage over the centralized, capital driven system of imported rice, which had replaced it. It was decentralized and close to the folks that used it. Neither money nor roads were required which was fortunate, as both were in short supply.

The point of this tale is not to celebrate the good old days, nor to idealize some romanticized notion of past tribal life. The lesson I perceive here is of the mind-boggling complexity of an apparently simple problem-solution scenario. What started out as a good idea at the time, to fix an obvious problem, dissolved into multiple new dilemmas. One cannot draw a straight line from the failed Swamp Rice project to the current sad situation of the Failed State of Liberia. But

there is no question that Liberia is a failed state, and I believe
no small part of that failure may be traced to an inability, or
unwillingness, to acknowledge the unbelievable complexity of
a situation, and the bluntness of our tools. Add in massive
doses of avarice and greed, and you have the perfect formula
for failure, which we achieved.

LESSONS LEARNED—A WHOLE SYSTEMS APPROACH

Almost 40 years have passed since I was in Liberia, and in the
interim we have learned a few things. Barriers to Peace remain
and, if anything, have increased in size. But their names
continue largely unchanged: hunger, ignorance, economic
deprivation, social injustice and dysfunction, and many more.
But it is now startlingly clear that none of these challenges to
the tranquility of the planet occur in isolation, they all have a
context which insures that the whole is infinitely greater than
the sum of the parts. That context, of course, is the social entity
afflicted, and that entity does not come in packages labeled
education, finance, social justice, economic development. The
names are something like New York, Monrovia, Dar Es
Salaam, Mogadishu and the like. Furthermore, all problem
areas are interrelated so that the parts are infinitely more
complex than they might appear at first sight. A "problem"
which initially looked like an Education Problem turns out to
be an education/economic/nutritional/social justice/etc.
problem. It becomes clear that one cannot deal with a part
without considering the whole, nor the whole without effectively dealing with the multiple interrelationships of the parts.
Mind bending, but there seems to be a way forward.

Coming out of the world of Systems Theory, ably articulated
by the likes of Peter Senge[7] the notion is a simple one. Parts

---

[7]   Senge, Peter, *The Fifth Discipline,* Doubleday/Currency, 1990.

only make sense in the context of the system of which they are a constituent element. And to understand what is going on in any significant area of human activity (as indeed all the rest of the cosmos) you have to think systemically. Senge's work was directed initially at the world of business and commerce, where he is probably best known as the originator of the Learning Organization, but the impact of Systems Thinking has been felt in virtually all areas of activity where the intent was to consider and enhance the complex machinations of the human community.

In the international development community (where a primary concern is, one hopes, Peacemaking) systems thinking shows up as Multi-Factorial Development. Thus when one is working in one of the hot spots of the world such as The Balkans, or the Middle East, it is understood from the start that educational interventions (for example) alone will have only limited effect unless combined with the whole broad range of developmental activities such as economic, infrastructure (roads and such), legal systems, public administration, and many more. Positively an elegant idea, but the passage from concept to successful implementation is blocked by extraordinary obstacles.

On a recent journey to Serbia, whose tribulations and needs appear almost unending, I had the privilege of working with a large international development program which was operating in the multi-factorial mode. Funded primarily by the United States Agency for International Development (USAID), the program had multiple elements all designed to work together in what might be described as *a full court press* [8]

---

[8] *Full Court Press* comes from the world of basket ball and refers to the strategy of attacking the opposing team from all sides (Full Court).

on the problems of that country. From economics to education with many pieces in between, the multi-factorial list had been checked off, and the pertinent programs put in place. A voluminous program plan minutely outlined the steps and relationships to be effected, all presented with mind boggling, complex detail. It looked marvelous on paper.

Since the overall program has only recently begun, any judgment regarding final impact is premature. But the early signs were hardly encouraging. Although the people involved seemed expert in their several areas, and used words like "cross disciplinary conversation and collaboration," at the end of the day, economists still seemed to think and act as economists, educators as educators, engineers as engineers and all of them thought like the expatriates they were. In short, it was not Serbian.

It is very easy to make such a critique, and my intent is not to disparage the concept, the energy and dedication of those involved, or the overall objectives. The concept is truly elegant, the people generally outstanding, and goodness knows the objectives, both in general and particular, are laudable. My issue quite simply is: can we get there from here going the way we are going? Simply, is it really possible to *think systemically* towards some useful conclusion? And having thought the thoughts, is it really possible to effectively weave the myriad elements into some coherent, new social fabric bearing the requisite characteristics of Peace, i.e., wholeness, health and harmony?

I would guess that the answer is yes, conceptually. However, execution to date has not been exactly outstanding, to the point that some senior officials in the United States government, including the President, George W. Bush, and the Secretary of the Treasury, Mr. Neil, came to the conclusion that the idea of Nation Building (development and Peacemaking on a truly grand scale) is off the agenda. I would disagree totally, but I can appreciate their position. For all of the billions of dollars expended since the end of World War II, the results have been disappointing, witness the current state of our world.

Others will suggest that given the stakes we are now facing, and no matter the experience to date, we simply have to keep trying. Perhaps someday we will get it right. I cannot disagree, but I would suggest that it might be well to take a look at our fundamental premises and explore the possibility of alternatives, or additions. *Putting it directly, is it really possible to think systemically and then rationally implement effective solutions, when the system we must think about is so horrendously complex as to boggle the mind, and the rapidity of change such that our best thoughts and efforts are rendered futile before the ink dries on the page, or the fingers leave the computer keyboard?*

We might imagine a day when our vaunted, and growing, capacity for digital wizardry increases to the extent that one might effectively model the whole system (Serbia, the Middle East, the total human community) in its totality and infinite detail, so that we actually see what is going on at all levels, from the whole enchilada down to the finest grain of rice. Then as conditions change, we could push that wonderful button, "Recalculate" and our cosmic spread sheet would supply the new picture. In that scenario, we would not be limited to historical data and present experience, for we could also play grand "What if?" games, postulating future occurrences and calculating possible results.

Advanced computer technology is not my field, and as a lay person I can only hope that such a happy day will soon arrive, but until then (or even after) I confess to certain reservations. Based on my very limited knowledge, it appears to me that the computer(s) required may give new meaning to the words Super Computer, and just the data entry needs would keep a small army of technicians at work for a long period. None of this is bad or impossible, but applied on a global scale, I would imagine the costs in terms of time and funds to be staggering, and unfortunately, both time and money seem to be in very short supply in our current quest for Peace.

DEEPER RESERVATIONS—HAVE WE THOUGHT ABOUT THE <u>WHOLE</u> SYSTEM?

The systemic approach to development, and ultimately Peacemaking, is an obvious advance over some of our earlier efforts. While the idea is a good one, I think there is real question as to whether or not we have gone far enough. Have we truly thought about the *whole system?*

Ken Wilber,[9] who is probably best known as a philosopher, psychologist, and mystic, argues, no. Indeed, he would suggest that we are playing with only half a deck of cards, thereby making the quality of our playing somewhat questionable. In very simple terms, Wilber proposes what appears to be self-evident, but with some interesting implications. He says that for every "outside" there is an "inside", and there are "outsides" and "insides" for groups (the collective) and for individuals. From this came what Wilber calls The Four Quadrant Systems Model. When we look at any system and its components, we typically start with the externals—the so called hard realities such as dollars earned, students educated,

---

[9] Ken Wilber is a prolific writer, but for an introduction to his thought, particularly as it relates to the issues under discussion here, I recommend *A Brief History of Everything,* published by Shambala in 1996. The title is outrageous, but in large part, I think Wilber delivers.

buildings built, roads traveled, and the like. This is quite understandable, if only because such things are what we can see and count. At some level, and for many people, if you can't "get a number on it" it doesn't quite exist. Starting with the externals is doubtless a good place to start, but it leaves the whole arena of internals unexamined. Internals would include such things as values and emotions. Thus knowing that there are X number of students in school tells you nothing about whether the education is "good," and what would *good* mean anyhow? Equally, you would know nothing about what the students felt about their learning; are they happy, sad, bored?

The examples given are oversimplified, and often much effort is devoted to "getting a number" on the interiors mentioned through questionnaires and focus groups. One might question how accurate such numbers might be, but that is really a different issue. However, I think Wilber's critique stands. The so called system thinkers appear much more comfortable with the hard "countables" than with what some would term the "warm fuzzies," and to the extent this is true, they are playing with only half a deck when it comes to looking at the whole system.

THE EVOLUTION OF CONSCIOUSNESS

The simplicities of Wilber's thinking quickly become complex when he adds the evolutionary dimension. We might avoid this complexity in our search for a Practice of Peace, save for the fact that I believe it presents our greatest challenge. More than the disparity of power and resources, or the presence, or absence of relevant social and physical infrastructure, I believe disparities in our individual and collective consciousness represent the critical hurdle for the Peacemaker. Therefore I beg your forbearance as we take a brief sojourn into the arcane world of Consciousness. It is my intent only to say enough to make the pertinent points, which will inevitably mean that my treatment of this enormous body of thought and experience will be superficial at best. For those who wish to go deeper, I will leave a trail of footnotes.

Along with many world thinkers, Wilber sees not only internals and externals in all human systems, but also an evolutionary progress of the human adventure such that both internals and externals change, or change their meaning, at each step along the journey. For example, if we may assume that individuals and organizations that see themselves as belonging to a Nation State somehow represent an advance over those who understand the world, and their place therein, in tribal terms, it should then be expected that the nature and content of Education, along with the meaning of the good, the true, and the beautiful might be quite different at each level of evolution.

The notion of some kind of hierarchy of consciousness, or awareness, has come in for rough treatment in recent times. Indeed it has become quite politically incorrect in some circles to even suggest that Tribal is somehow inferior to Nation State. It is pointed out that many aspects of tribal life have much to teach us in the modern world of the nation state. I myself made exactly this point in a short book on Liberian tribal life.[10] That said, I think few would argue with the notion that tribal life, as we see it manifest in our world, or know it from the ancient artifacts and literature, has a few drawbacks we would just as soon do without. But our evolutionary progression (which I take to be real) is no justification for the rather smug notion of the 19th century Doctrine of

___
[10] *When the Devil Dances,* Mara Books, 1970.

Progress, which held that everything is just getting better and better. Obviously, some things have gotten better, and equally some things have gotten worse. Take for example our knowledge of the atom's secrets, which has enabled great progress in the practice of medicine, and also made possible the total annihilation of the human species. Rather than a march of inevitable progress, our experience is much closer to the ancient understanding of light and shadow. The greater the light, the deeper the shadow. There are real gains and deeper possibilities for destruction.

There are innumerable and sometimes enormously detailed versions of the evolution of consciousness. The model that Wilber presents through his All Quadrant work is an elegant piece of detailed scholarship, a wonder in itself, but perhaps more complex than we need at the moment in order to see the relevant points and move on to the practicalities of peacemaking. A sparser version is offered by Don Beck and Christopher Cowan under the banner of Spiral Dynamics,[11] but it too has a level of detail I feel to be unneeded at the moment. For our purposes, I think we can do well with what might be termed the original version, which is traditionally known as *The Great Chain of Being.*

Wilber himself uses this millennia old model in some of his earlier works[12] and I will use his version. Traditionally there are understood to be seven levels to our increasing consciousness. The first level is "nothing," as is the last. Since it is quite difficult to speak of "nothing" we are left with the remaining five, which are Body, Mind, Intellect, Soul, and

---

[11] Beck, Don Edward and Christopher C. Cowan, *Spiral Dynamics: Mastering Values, Leadership, and Change (Developmental Management).*

[12] Wilber, Ken, *Up From Eden,* Anchor Press Doubleday, 1981.

Spirit. Very roughly, these levels of consciousness may be described as follows.

We all start at the level of *Body,* and the extent of our awareness goes scarcely further than the tip of our nose. We might think of the newborn child, or small infant, for whom the world is its *corpus delicti,* and major concerns of the day include eating and the opposite. Of course, creature comforts, such as hugs and kisses are nice too. It might be noted that all of us start here, and there is nothing wrong, or bad, with that status, unless we never grow out of it, which most of us do.

Next stop is the level of *Mind.* Here we develop certain mental capacities, the major one being language, which enables us to engage a wider world in ways other than the purely physical. Words and realities coalesce so that we can perceive differences and identity. Thus "Mommy or Daddy" takes some shape in our awareness as something special and unique. As our vocabulary grows so does our perception of the world, and at this stage our perception is our reality. All very good, and a definite improvement over life as Body, but not without limitations, especially when it comes to making critical assessments, and reasoning our way through life. Just think of a three year old with lots of new words and marginal judgment. Fortunately, there is more.

The fourth level of consciousness is *Intellect,* which might also be understood as the consciousness of consciousness. This is that point in our development when we find the capacity to think critically about our state and our future. This is also the point where our Ego comes into play. And so *I* (as distinct from all else and others) can look critically at my self and my world to contemplate its goodness or badness, while simultaneously raising the possibility that it could be better. In short, the future comes into play, and it seems possible to influence the course of that future to my advantage. Pretty heady stuff. And there is the rub. We tend to get stuck in our heads, and hung up in the ego. This is the proverbial good news/bad news situation. As we become critical of our situation (good news), we may become overly critical and think we are in charge (bad news). But there is hope.

Hope appears with the next level in our journey to consciousness. Call it *Soul*. Soul, as I am using it here, has little to do with that disembodied something we never quite get our hands on, and rather more to do with American Black street usage, as in *"He/she got Soul."* If I hear my black friends correctly, this translates to mean, "He/she has it all together." It seems this is about the full integration, and transcendence of the prior three levels. We still have Body, Mind and Intellect, but now they are all working together, and best of all, we can now find our rightful place in the world at large, not as an alien, stranger or combatant hiding behind thick walls of ego, but as a co-sojourner in the cosmos, one amongst the many critters. We are fully integrated, and fully individual, with a proper sense of place and purpose. No longer the "wannabe" ruler of the universe seeking personal command and control at all costs (dominion over the earth), but a good and responsible cosmic citizen.

And the journey is not yet complete, for tradition tells us that there is yet another level to be attained: *Spirit*. In rather esoteric terms this might be described as consciousness appearing as itself, pure consciousness no longer constrained by the normal limitations of time and space. Granted, such a state of consciousness is hard to talk about, and may be even hard to imagine. However, I think there are some elements of our common experience that give us useful clues, such as those rare and wonderful moments when we find ourselves performing at levels well in excess of our technical ability, or even physical possibility. Athletes call this *Being in the Zone*, and Jazz musicians call it *Being in the Groove*. By whatever name, and no name really does it, this is Peak Performance (Maslow) with a vengeance.

There is one final piece to be added to this schema, at least in the view of Ken Wilber, which I share. *Each level transcends and includes the preceding one(s)*. Thus if one were to represent the evolution graphically, the appropriate picture would be not a ladder, but rather nested spheres. As we move from Body to Mind, we don't loose Body; rather it is transcended and included by Mind. And also at the level of Intellect, we do not remove Body or Mind, but both are effectively out-framed, and included in the new consciousness of whom and what we are. The importance of this additional piece is that no matter what level of consciousness we attain, we always have available that which came before, which may be understood as primal or deeper.

With the arrival of the level of Spirit, we come to the end of the journey of consciousness described by age old tradition. I leave it to your further reading to explore the details and philosophical underpinnings, or if you are already deeply grounded in the experience, and wish to debate the fine points, I beg deferral to another time. For the moment I would like to suggest that even if the words and descriptions don't quite fit, there is a certain intuitive "rightness" to the descriptions as offered. There should be little problem with the levels of Body, Mind, and Intellect. We all recognize the territory and the associated benefits and liabilities. Things get a little fuzzier once we reach Soul and Spirit, but even here I suspect we can all feel a certain connectedness. We know people who seem to have it all together, and yet remain open to new experience and possibility. And we have at least heard of folks who make it to the *Zone*. So if "intuitive rightness" works for you, it will be a more than sufficient basis from which to make a most important point. One implication of this hierarchy (and yes, it is a hierarchy, but so are all developmental taxonomies from Aristotle to Piaget, and onwards), is the potential for genuine misunderstanding, conflict and confusion. It pretty much comes with the territory—probably can't be avoided, and even has some real benefit—but it should be of genuine concern to all those who would follow the path of Peacemaking, at least at the level of interpersonal relationships.

CONFLICTS OF CONSCIOUSNESS—THE INDIVIDUAL

The simple truth of the matter is that individuals separated by more than two levels of consciousness have real problems with each other, and actually even those on adjoining levels are not very comfortable. For example, those at the level of *Intellect* find the behavior of those at the Body level annoying at the least, and probably boorish, particularly if the Intellectual has gotten locked in the person's ego, which is a constant danger. Of course, if the offending party is a small baby allowances can be made, maybe. But should the offender be an adult (and in truth many adults never quite get beyond the Body level of consciousness), that individual is definitely off the list, to be avoided at all costs, and if encountered then subjected to the strictest of controls. Such people are called stupid, or more colorfully, "Hunks" (for the guys) and "Dolls" (for the women). All Body, no brains (mind), and not a shred of intellect anywhere. And this is the stuff of good relationships?

On the other side of the fence, the situation is no less contentious. For the Body who, please note, is quite happy to be Body, and for whom the ultimate life experience may be defined as a cold Budweiser in hand on a warm sandy beach—Intellect is a dreadful snob. And that is putting it mildly. Given sufficient language skills, which are not typically present, the description would go on to include words like effete, party-pooper, and subversive. Under normal circumstances, Body will never meet Intellect, but in the unhappy event that they do, a good punch in the nose might straighten things out. Thus, we have a problem, particularly if our concern is for making and keeping Peace.

And just to make matters a little worse, consider another unhappy circumstances which may arise between two individuals one level apart, in this case Intellect and Soul. Not only do they see themselves and their worlds in vastly different ways, it is also true that the *summum bonum* of each is anathema to the other. For Intellect, control and being in control are viewed as life's highest calling, and to be out of control is to be consigned to the dung heap of history. This fixation on control may be relatively benign so long as the threat level is low, and it appears that all is in order, which means that I am in charge, or at the very least somebody I know and trust is in charge. But as the threat level increases, so does the urge to control.

Soul, on the other hand has a very different view of control, at least the sort of control idolized by Intellect. Soul recognizes that this absolute, being-in-charge sort of control is basically a figment of a fertile imagination, or more accurately, a deluded ego. It is not so much bad as illusory, given the complexity of things and the capricious nature of change.

But the *quest* for such control is understood to be highly destructive because of the way it is carried out. Operating under the ancient maxim of "Divide and Conquer," Intellect segregates the elements of his/her world into smaller and smaller pieces, which are contained in smaller and smaller spaces. This is justified initially in terms of understanding how things work, otherwise known as making intellectual distinctions. The model for this behavior is the procedure of dissection. Thus to know (understand) a frog, one cuts it in small pieces. At the end of the day, Intellect perceives an advance in knowledge, and a gain in control (over frogs). Soul on the other hand sees primarily a small pile of pieces, and the destruction of life.

In the unhappy event that Soul and Intellect are forced to work together, or worse yet, that one or the other is assigned the role of "supervisor," the two are in for some rough water. While Intellect is busy making distinctions by building departments, bureaus, and branches all separated by clean lines of authority and responsibility, which are maintained and enforced by a vigilant management, all in the name of control, Soul has a very different agenda.

For Soul, life and organization become fully meaningful and functional only in their totality and wholeness, and while differences and separations do occur, they are to be linked and bridged to enable a natural, organic flow. The keywords are integration and wholeness. For Intellect, the keys are separation and control. It usually does not take long before we hear Soul mumbling something about fascist dictator, while Intellect decries the muddleheaded idealist. Not a positive working environment.

Under circumstances like those just described, which often become increasingly uncomfortable and destructive for the individuals involved, it is tempting to find a fix—typically some form of mediation or negotiation, based upon a rational approach which seeks understanding of all positions. This is a fine idea, but doomed to failure from the start, for rational conversation requires, at a minimum, the sharing of some fundamental, common presuppositions. In these situations, those common presuppositions do not exist. All individuals look at themselves and the world from their own point of view which is determined by their level of consciousness. What is logical and rational from the viewpoint of Body (more beer and a better beach) makes no connection with the premises of Intellect, which might be something like "finer distinctions and more productive control." It is a classic case of apples and oranges.

With failure of a negotiated settlement, a more radical strategy is employed which might be termed Separation of the Parties. Since it appears that there are irreconcilable differences and little basis for common understanding, it only makes sense to put some distance between the folks in the name of organizational tranquility (which should not be confused with Peace). Under this plan, only Body types may play on the beach, Intellectuals should talk to each other, and Souls should be left to wander the fields of wholeness. In truth such separation appears to occur as a natural phenomenon in our experience. We even have a short aphorism to describe the phenomenon, "Birds of a feather flock together." There is a short-term positive effect of this, but longer term, the results are hardly useful, for in place of the rich natural diversity of the human community the disparate elements are rigidly separated. Body folks are left on the beach with no challenge to move on. And

Intellectuals converse in their ivory towers, disengaged from the messiness of daily living.

A final strategy, which is draconian but unfortunately quite common, is the subjugation of the lower levels by the higher. The Body people are consigned to the shipping room and assembly line, Mind folks are expected to perform clerical tasks, and low level technical work, leaving Executive and Senior Management firmly in the hands of the Intellectuals. The arrangement has all the appearances of total order, and rigid discipline, to say nothing of tight command and control, all exercised to insure that order is maintained. It is surprising how long this dictatorial approach can be maintained, but occasionally it is challenged by a strike, or something similar, which the Intellectuals see as chaos, confusion and conflict.

As should be obvious, my description of the roles and relationships of the several levels of consciousness has been accomplished with great overstatement and little attention to details. I hope, however, that you will not be put off by the overly emphatic representations, but rather consider the possibilities inherent in what I have chosen to call *Conflicts of Consciousness.* Truthfully, there is nothing subtle about the intensity of engagement, or the damage that may be done. If our chosen role in life is that of Peace Maker, none of this can be overlooked. To be effective, it is essential that we deal not only with the bits and pieces of life, but also the wholeness of life, inside and out, and along the full spectrum of evolving consciousness. Obviously this is no small task, but before we can get to work, there is one additional level of complexity to be explored, which might be called the evolution of consciousness at the level of the organization. Or put as a question: What happens when individuals, at a particular level of consciousness, clump? If birds of a feather do indeed flock together, and if there are a large number of people with a common level of consciousness in a single organization, could it be that organizations as a whole have consciousness (collective consciousness), and therefore levels of consciousness?

ORGANIZATIONAL CONSCIOUSNESS

In the early 1980s, inspired by the work of Ken Wilber and driven by my own professional concerns to understand the deep functions of the organizations with which I worked, I found myself asking the question, *What are the organizational analogues to the individual levels of consciousness?*[13] It seems that other people, notably Ken Wilber and Don Beck, have been asking similar questions, but the history of this particular endeavor is a short one indeed, and definitely not to be compared with the age old consensus enjoyed by The Great Chain of Being. Regardless, the notion that there has occurred, in the process of human history, a certain unfolding of developmental stages is by no means novel. Historians, political scientists, sociologists, to say nothing of philosophers and priests, have all noticed and described in various terms the obvious (at least I think it is obvious) journey and way stations that *Homo sapiens* has traversed from the days of the primal pair to the present moment. The terms vary with the author, but the sequence usually goes something like Family, Clan, Tribe, Kingdom, Nation State, which seemingly brings us to the present moment.

---

[13] My early foray into the world of organizational consciousness is described in my first book, *Spirit: Transformation and Development in Organizations,* Abbott Publishing, 1987. This book is no longer in print, but an updated version appears in *The Power of Spirit: How Organizations Transform,* Berrett-Koehler, 2000.

From this moment forwards, the visionaries take over with projections for our future, which might include a Global State, or maybe the elimination of all States.

Settling the issues of the nature and levels of organizational consciousness will not be accomplished here, but I raise it only to suggest that if it all makes some sense, the job of the Peacemaker becomes profoundly interesting, to say nothing of difficult. As long as the threats to Peace through what I have called Conflicts of Consciousness exist only at the level of the individual, we have a problem, but it is one we can get our arms around, if only conceptually. The way forward, it would seem, lies in facilitating individual transformations until sufficient critical mass has been created in order to move the whole. When, however, the object of our concern ceases to be the individual and becomes whole organizations, countries, and cultures, we have a horse of a very different color. Dealing with the 6 billion-plus folks, currently existent on Planet Earth in all of their organizational aggregations, one person at a time, is mind boggling. And thinking about dealing with this mass of humanity all at once, simply goes off the charts. If the way forward lies through individual transformation with supportive therapy for those on the fringes, we will definitely have a shortage of ashrams and couches. And the notion of getting the whole system in the room, to quote the current mantra of those involved with large systems change, can only inspire an embarrassed chuckle.

CHAPTER III

Scope of Work for the Peacemaker

We began our exploration of The Practice of Peace with a short definition: *Peace is the dynamic interrelationship of complex forces productive of wholeness, health and harmony. The Practice of Peace is the intentional creation of the requisite conditions under which Peace may occur.*

Since that point, we have looked at some of the elements that constitute the playing field of Peacemaking, suggesting that the job neither begins nor ends at the negotiating table, but rather consists of the entire array of human activities, needs and services which conspire to create the conditions of meaningful life for all of us. Education, economics, agriculture, markets, arts, and on, and on, and on…And that is just to name the externals. All are necessary, but only a part of the equation. To this unending list we must add the "interiors" (the good, the true, the beautiful) and how each of the 6 billion of us feels about them at any given point in time.

And the playing field only gets rougher, for it appears that over time all of us are on a journey from very primal states of consciousness to deeper and more expanded understandings of who and what we are. With each step along the way, our perception of the good, the true, and the beautiful changes with our passage, as also our understanding of the perhaps more basic realities of life such as our jobs, and what makes for a "good one." Add into this swirling kaleidoscope of life the seemingly inevitable conflicts and misunderstandings arising from the differing perspectives of our several levels of consciousness (Body folks just don't "get" Intellectuals, and Intellectuals wouldn't give Body folks the time of day) and we have a very interesting stew.

And last but by no means least, should it turn out to be true that organizations (companies, countries, cultures) like individuals also have differing levels of consciousness which not only change over time, but at any given time may find themselves in conflict with their fellows, the scene becomes infinitely murkier. It seems that tribal folks are uncomfortable with kingdoms, and both tribes and kingdoms distrust the nation state. And all three are horrified by the encroachment of globalization, whether that is The Global State or the global inter-connectedness of Internet. Tribes are marginalized, kingdoms (and kings) loose their authority, and the nation state discovers its pride and joy—sovereignty—sitting on the slippery slope of oblivion. And the job of the Peacemaker is to put all of this together? Compared to such a task, reassembling Humpty Dumpty was a piece of cake!

IT'S ALL CONNECTED

If we have learned anything at all from Systems Thinking, it is that everything is connected. Nothing, no matter how minor, how apparently trivial, sits in splendid isolation. John Donne counseled us, "No man is an island entire of itself; every man is a piece of the Continent, a part of the main…[14] But with our current wisdom, we can take Donne's thought further, right down to the last atom, quark, or string. It is all part of the whole. Further, a change in any part will change the whole, because it is all connected. The fact that the change may be so infinitesimal as to be unnoticed doesn't alter the situation, and presuming the Complexity (Chaos) theorists have it right, a tiny change in a tiny part can have a major impact. After all, the wing flap of a butterfly in Saigon can change the weather patterns in California, or so the story goes.

---

[14] John Donne (c. 1572–1631), English divine and metaphysical poet. *Devotions Upon Emergent Occasions,* Meditation 17 (1624).

So there we have it. Incredible complexity, mind boggling diversity, and everything interconnected in ways that enables each part to affect all other parts, and therefore the whole. And if everything would just stand still we might, at least conceptually, get a reasonable handle on things. But it seems that not only is everything inter-connected, worse yet, everything is moving. Now what?

THE TOOLS OF PEACEMAKING

The tools of Peacemaking, as we might see them at the moment, are multiple. They range from the very narrow and specific approaches of conflict resolution and negotiation to the broadest interventions which target the larger, problematic elements of our life together including education, economic development, and the whole range of "nation building" efforts. When Peacemaking focuses on business and other organizations, the tools are similar, but with different names, such as training, development, financial planning etc. But for all their diversity and multiplicity, the several tools in the Peacemaker's kit share a common linage, at least in the West: Rational Analysis and Problem Solving. Regardless of the size or complexity of the issue confronting us, we follow a procedure which goes roughly as follows: 1) Data Collection 2) Rational Analysis 3) Problem Definition 4) Intervention Design 5) Application/Intervention 6) Evaluation. The actual steps may vary with situations. Some may be left out, and new ones can be added. And the whole thing may be done well, or poorly, but at the end of the day it all seems to come down to the same thing: Define the problem, fix it and demonstrate a return on investment.

There also seems to be a tendency to cut the problem down to some manageable size under the general rubric of eating the elephant one bite at a time. This makes a great deal of sense considering the size and complexity of the issues we face. However there is an unintended consequence. The more we isolate a particular problem situation, the narrower our view of the actual and potential interrelationships be they negative or positive. In worst case scenarios we discover that while we may have fixed the problem in view, we have created a dozen more, all worse than the problem we solved.

The results of our collective efforts have been impressive, but perhaps not for the reasons we might anticipate. There is no question that our capacity for data collection and analysis has improved over time. We typically unearth an infinity of facts, and our analytical abilities permit us to create fabulous maps of the size, shape, and elements of the problems we confront. However, when it comes to the critical execution of solutions, the record is not so outstanding. Lord knows we have tried, and when one effort fails, we try again, collecting more data, doing finer analysis, and creating more detailed solutions.

Perhaps it is time to recognize that it is not that we are doing something wrong, as in insufficient data collection, flawed analysis or poor design. Rather, we are doing the wrong thing. In a word, the difficulty lies with our method and approach, and not with the application. There is no question that our approach, which we might generally refer to as Rational Analysis, clearly reveals the scope and complexity of the problems we face. I believe it also reveals its own impotence for the resolution of these problems.

Putting all of this in more personal terms, I note that many of my colleagues and friends take great pride and pleasure in their rigorous collection of data, the clarity of their analysis, and the elegance of their models—believing that all of this will lead to good and effective solutions. Such efforts have their place, but the net result for me is something approaching despair. I feel overwhelmed by the data, claustrophobic with the models, and exhausted by the proposed solutions. Doubtless this is the result of a simple mind and waning energy, but I conclude that going the way we are going is a certain prescription for not arriving at our intended destination: The realization of Peace. The alternatives, as I see them at the moment, are either give in to despair, or find a better way. I have no argument with the obvious need for adequate and accurate data, detailed analysis, or elegant models, for all of this presents us with a clear vision of the problems we face. But when it comes to resolution, we desperately need something infinitely more powerful than the meager tools in hand. And in the meantime, we might consider the fact that in spite of everything, we are still surviving on planet Earth. As the British might say, we are "muddling through."

CHAPTER IV
Muddling Through

The British, long known for their stiff upper lip and a seeming capacity for getting it right and doing things "correctly," have another side which they display when it all falls apart and yet somehow victory is snatched from the jaws of defeat, often for no apparent reason. They call it "muddling through." So as we look at the problems of our non-pacific world, and concede the apparent powerlessness of the tools at our disposal, it may be well to reflect on the fact that despite a continuing history which appears anything but whole, healthy and harmonious, to say nothing of peaceful—we are still here. Further, on any given day, not withstanding multiple wars and rumors of wars, all combined with famine, plague and pestilence, a sizable proportion of the citizens of Plant Earth seem to be getting on with life. In short, we muddle through.

One might argue, as indeed I would be happy to, that "muddling through" is a rather dismal condition for creatures whose potential is as vast as our own. Somehow it should all be better! Yet, just for the moment, consider how good it is, and has been. Think of the glass as half full, and not half empty.

A million years ago or so, our ancestors were hiding out in caves if they were lucky. Lunch wandered by on the hoofs of passing hairy Mammoths, and if you could dodge the competing Saber Toothed Tigers, you might get a slice. Then again, you might be the luncheon special.

A professional paleontologist would doubtless take issue with the accuracy of my scenario, but I think the point still stands; we have come a long way. Caves have given way to villages, towns, cities, and now megalopolis. Pigeons and smoke signals have been replaced by Internet. And lunch can typically be found at the corner bistro, chop shop, or market stall. Is it perfect? Definitely not, but I don't hear too many folks celebrating the good old days in The Cave, dodging the Saber Tooth, and munching on Mammoth.

It is a reasonable question to ask: How did all this come about? We might like to imagine a Strategic Planning Committee convened in some central cave, plotting the future course of Humankind. This would certainly fit in with our current understanding of how such things would get done. To listen to the conventional wisdom, it appears that nothing can happen until it is planned, organized, executed and evaluated. So obviously there had to be somebody in the Executive Suite somewhere.

More recently it seems that The Supreme Executive Committee, at least its latest iterations, has fallen on hard times. They may have the vision, mission and goals down pat, but when it comes to organization and execution, there appears to be a notable glitch. But isn't it wonderful that we have done as well as we have? Personally, I take it as a major miracle that we are actually here to complain about how bad things have become. Somebody did something right somewhere!

It might also be worthwhile noting that the closer we come to our own time, the worse things seem to become. Looking back over the stream of human history, you don't have to be a Pollyannaish optimist to perceive a wonderful tapestry of evolving life. To be sure there are some holes in the fabric, and more than a few delightful patterns that seem to run out of steam, and disappear at the edges. But as a whole, and on the whole, the species we call *Homo sapiens* is pretty remarkable.

THE LONG VIEW

It has been often observed that the human experiment, at least in terms of time, can be compared to the skin on Mother Nature's teeth. Very thin and of recent vintage. What's a few million years compared to the 14 billion since it all began, at least according to the scientific community. Long ago and far away there was indeed a shot heard around the cosmos. In one fiery instant we apparently went from nothing to something, and it has been spreading out ever since. Superheated cosmic plasma cooled to allow the appearance of electrons and quarks that mated to create atoms and molecules, all illuminating glowing gas clouds, which congealed into clumps. Galaxies, stars, planets, moons, asteroids, all spread across inter-galactic space. Pretty good show. And somewhere in all of this we showed up on a minor galaxy, behind a second rate star, hiding out on a small piece of solar driftwood. Big deal. Well, it is a big deal—for us.

Now back to the original question. How did all this happen? One traditional answer, of course, is that God did it. I have no basic argument with such an answer, but it still seems reasonable to ask how did He or She pull it off? We might, for example say that God created life, but that still leaves plenty of room for sex in the process. The answer in this case is almost embarrassingly simple. *It happened all by itself.* Well, almost.

IT HAPPENED ALL BY ITSELF—ALMOST

Over the past 30 years, there has emerged in the scientific community a surprising consensus that the fundamental principle in the creation of the cosmos and its creatures (including us) is Self-organization. Given certain, very simple pre-conditions it seems that order emerges from chaos. The precise definition of these pre-conditions is a matter of continuing discovery—accompanied by no small amount of debate. But the general idea of Self-organization has clearly taken a firm hold in the minds of many scientists, and should their suspicion turn to conviction, which in turn is confirmed over time by the rigorous application of scientific discipline, our basic understanding of ourselves, our world, and the cosmos of which we are all a part will take on a very different aspect.

Telling this tale in its fullness is not something I am competent to do, nor does this present book provide the space. Fortunately the tale is being told by many others whose work I will use and acknowledge. For me, the story begins with the efforts of Ilya Prigogine reported in his 1980 book *From Being to Becoming,* and again in his 1984 book, *Order Out of Chaos.*[15] I have no idea whether Prigogine was the first to articulate the notion of Self-organization, and some historian of science may be grappling with this question as you read this. But Prigogine grabbed my attention with his then-revolutionary idea of "Dissipative Structures." I am obviously a tardy student, for Prigogine had already grabbed the attention of the scientific community, witness his 1977 Nobel Prize in chemistry, but his thought was simple, profound, and for me, mind blowing. Baldly stated, Prigogine's work with chemical systems, including such mundane systems as a tea kettle on the stove, suggested to him that when such systems are driven "far out of equilibrium" due to changed environmental circumstances (the heat is turned on under the kettle) the initial response is pure chaos. The placid water in the pot manifests random swirls and bubbles. Things get worse until suddenly chaotic randomness is replaced by new and more complex order. In the case of the kettle, it is tea time, for we now have a beautiful rolling boil!

---

[15] Prigogine, Iilyaa, *Being and Becoming,* W. H. Freeman, 1980.
_____*Order Out of Chaos,* Bantam Books, 1984.

Order appears in chaos. Nobody did it. Not a committee or executive in sight, but things definitely get organized at a new and higher level of complexity. But, you say quite correctly, it is only a tea kettle. How about systems of a different sort and larger systems?

James Gleick in his book, *Chaos: Making a New Science*[16] takes the tale of Self-organization in a new and interesting direction by exploring a remarkable "underground operation" that apparently began as early as 1960 with the strange discoveries of Edward Lorenz. Lorenz was a meteorologist who was understandably fascinated by weather, or more exactly the changeableness of weather. Like all weather forecasters, he dreamed of finding the patterns so that real prediction might be possible. Using a very primitive (as we would see it now) computer, he modeled a weather system in simple terms, pushed the button, and when the computer ran (it often broke down), out came a nicely evolving system with recognizable patterns of pressure and temperature, always slightly different, but definitely in a comfortable pattern. Prediction of the sort that would make any forecaster proud seemed a real possibility.

Pushing his luck, he took a closer look at the computer generated system, and to save a little time, he started a new "run" by entering the final numbers from the previous one. He went out for coffee, and upon his return discovered that his nice, orderly patterns had become something totally new. How could it be? Same computer, same program, same numbers—but very different results. A definite mystery. It turned out that in re-entering the numbers, Lorenz had dropped 3 of 6 decimal places, feeling that a difference of slightly more than one part in a thousand would make little

---

[16] Gleick, James, *Chaos: Making a New Science,* Viking Penguin, 1987.

difference. How wrong he was! But with such mistakes major learning becomes possible, even when that learning is decidedly uncomfortable. The meteorologist's dream of tight predictions would have to wait for another day, but for the moment the insight was fantastic. It turns out that in open systems (and the weather system is definitely open), the tiniest of changes can have major impacts. The Butterfly Effect had been discovered.

The pursuit of Chaos in all its forms became a phenomenon with the appearance of a remarkable group of scientists at the Santa Cruz campus of the University of California. According to Gleick, the group called itself the "Dynamical Systems Collective." Others apparently referred to it in less laudatory terms as, "The Chaos Cabal." By whatever name, the group, lead by Robert Shaw, a young graduate student, was covering ground few had traversed previously, and many would not wish to walk, if only because the experience repre-sented a profound challenge to the notion of predictability which the sciences found to be so comfortable. When random flaps of butterfly wings (metaphorically) can send a system off in new and unpredictable directions, the clockwork notion of the universe of Newtonian days was in deep trouble. It was indeed a strange new world. And it would get stranger.

Chaos had long been held to be the enemy of all that is good, true and beautiful, and when the world was working perfectly, Chaos was absent. And should Chaos rear its ugly head, the job of all right thinking people, was to eliminate it quickly. But now it seemed, at least to Shaw and his colleagues, chaos had a positive contribution to make to the process of life. Gleick summarizes their emerging understanding as follows, "Chaos was the creation of information."[17] Unraveling the technicalities of that gnomic statement would take us well beyond the scope of this book and, frankly, my competence. My point, however, is a simple one. Chaos was now to be understood as an integral part of the process of living. No longer the devil incarnate, it was becoming clear that chaos had its uses—positive and essential uses.

What was also becoming clear is that chaos (and Chaos Theory) was only part of the equation. The real news was that chaos had an order, or maybe that order appeared in chaos. Or perhaps best of all, that beings (animate and inanimate, large and small, cosmic and creaturely) emerge in a dance between chaos and order. Never fully chaotic, never completely ordered, always on the way. In this light it would seem that the title of Gleick's book (*Chaos*) was actually a misnomer. It is not just Chaos. Nor is it just order. It is the complex inter-relationship between the two.

COMPLEX ADAPTIVE SYSTEMS AND THE SANTA FE INSTITUTE

The Santa Fe Institute is a marvelous institution populated by world class scientists, many of whom came originally from the nearby Los Alamos laboratory. Their passion is Self-organizing Systems which they have been studying at virtually all levels and scales, beginning with the sub atomic realms, which is the peculiar domain of Murray Gell-Mann, another Nobel Laureate, and one of the most illustrious members of the Institute. Actually Gell-Mann takes the full trip from the most elemental "bits"—the quark, which was his contribution to the amazing world of physics—up to and

---

[17] *Op cit* pg 260.

including the entire cosmos.[18] And if Gell-Mann is to be believed, it is all one big self-organizing system, which in the terms common to the Institute is denominated a Complex Adaptive System. *Complex,* in that it is composed of multiple and diverse pieces in differing relationships, *Adaptive,* in that the system is constantly "learning" new and effective means to fit with its environment in ways that honor its wholeness and enable a healthy, harmonious existence. And *System* in the sense that it actually works together.

ORDER FOR FREE

"Order for Free" is the mantra of Stuart Kauffman, or at least it seems that way, for the phrase appears as a recurrent theme in his book, *At Home in the Universe.*[19] Kauffman is a biologist and a colleague of Gell-Mann at the Santa Fe Institute. His life passion is to understand the mechanisms by which we, and all other living creatures, emerged from the primal soup. On the face of it, this appears as a most improbable journey. Once upon a time, Planet Earth was a scorching hot solar cast-off, spinning quietly in space. Odd atoms and molecules populated the surface, creating a lethal brew—definitely not hospitable for living creatures as we know them. Then somehow, someway, this lethal brew was stirred in a fashion such that life appeared, and after some long time, we showed up—you and me and all the other 6 billion of us, as well as all the other creatures of the Earth. And how, pray tell, did that happen? Kauffman's answer, very much in line with others who contemplate the mystery of self-organization, it happened all by itself. Or in his words, "Order for Free."

---

[18] Gell-Mann, Murray, *The Quark and the Jaguar,* W.H.Freeman, 1994.

[19] Kauffman, Stuart, *At Home in the Universe,* Oxford University Press, 1995.

Based upon his research with computer models and in the laboratory, Kauffman has concluded that given certain very simple pre-conditions, the process of self-organization commences and, at the end of the day—indeed at the end of many days—the complex chemistry of life is in place and the show can begin. Needless to say, I must leave any judgment as to the correctness of Kauffman's proposals in the competent hands of his peers. However, judging from the attributions and footnotes appearing in various scientific books and journals it is clear that while the jury is still out on the adequacy of the details, a growing number of scientists appear to believe that Kauffman is heading in the right direction.

I think I have it right that the pre-conditions Kauffman describes are as follows:

1) A relatively safe, nutrient environment.

2) High levels of diversity of elements, and the potential for complex inter-relationships.

3) A drive for improvement (search for fitness).

4) Sparse prior connections.

5) Edge of chaos.

A relatively safe, nutrient environment. The process of self-organization can only begin when there is some degree of safety and support in the overall environment. In terms of the early moments, back in the days of primal soup, this might mean that the shadow of a kindly rock protected the soon-to-be organized elements from the devastating blast of solar radiation. Things might be bad elsewhere, but for a moment there was a safe harbor.

High levels of diversity of elements, and the potential for complex inter-relationships. The second precondition is that the elements in the soup be diverse (not all one thing) and that among them there exists the potential for complex interrelationships.

A drive for improvement (search for fitness.) A drive for improvement is a rather inelegant, and possibly misleading, way to describe a central force in evolutionary theory, the search for fitness. The notion, however, is probably simpler than the words. We are talking about looking for a better way to be. So, for example, if you are an atom, it is somehow better to connect to another atom, thereby becoming a molecule, especially if that union allows for a better (more competitive, more secure) relationship with the environment. Likewise, two simple molecules might find life better if they were to join and form a complex molecule. Anthropomorphizing atoms is dangerous if only because it might seem that I am attributing consciousness to these electronic wonders. That is not my intent (although who knows what the real situation might be) however the net effect, whether conscious or not, is to move in the direction of increased complexity as a way of more adequately existing in the world. This is the age old quest to fit in, belong, find a home in the universe, as Kauffman might say.

Sparse prior connections. The point here is that the to-be-self-organized elements should have few, if any, prior connections if they are going to organize in new and more effective ways. The fewer the prior connections the higher the likelihood of productive novelty. Put in terms appropriate to the world of computers, if the whole thing is "hardwired" at the start, the possibility of new associations is limited indeed, short of tearing all the pre-existing wiring out.

Edge of chaos. Here is the "kicker." The whole mess, whatever that mess, must be what folk singer James Taylor called a "churning urn of boiling funk."[20] He was talking about his emotional condition in the presence of his beloved, but just as new relationships seem to require the messiness of passion at their start, so also the process towards organization. If everything is just sitting there like an inert blob, not too much will happen. The essential presence of chaos in the process of ordering puts a whole new light on our ancient nemesis. Far from being the enemy of organization, it should now be seen as an essential precondition. No chaos, no order, no life.

Doubtless Kauffman's list of essential preconditions will change as he, and a multitude of others, dive deeper into this incredible (as some would see it) mystery. But if there is lack of agreement on the details, there is little question that the central concept is gaining massive support. Despite the skepticism engendered by much of our current theory and practice of organization, it appears that getting organized is no big, complex, effort-intensive deal. Given the right (simple) conditions, organization happens all by itself and (just about) everywhere. Order for free.

Ants, Brains and Cities

Self-organizing systems, it would appear, show up just about anywhere: the minute world of ants, the mind numbing complexity of the human brain, and in humankind's larger efforts, the city. Steven Johnson, in his book, *Emergence*[21] pulls together the work of many people to make just this point.

---

[20] Taylor, James, *Steamroller,* Country Road Music/Blackwood Music Inc. BMI, 1970.

[21] Johnson, Steven, *Emergence: the Connected Lives of Ants, Brains and Cities,* Scribner, 2001.

Have you ever wondered how it might be that the humble ant, with scarcely a brain in its tiny head, could manage to pull of such marvels of architectural genius as the ant hill with its multiple chambers and varied functions? Not a design team in sight, nor engineers, project planners, managers, or any of the other accouterments that accompany human efforts of this sort. And yet, billions of times over millions of years, the little critters did it. And how was that? You guessed it—self-organization one more time. Following very simple rules established as the preconditions of their life together, the millions of creatures do collectively what not one of them could even imagine.

Or how about the human brain, that incredible collection of neurons and synapses, which on the surface looks like nothing more than pudgy grey cauliflower, and yet is obviously capable of recording and analyzing this piece about Peace, and much, much more. How did it ever get put together, and how does it do as well as it does, albeit with few lapses here and there? The answer according to those who study such things is that the brain, like all the rest of creation it would seem, works because self-organization works.

The power of self-organization seemingly manifests itself in all the nooks and crannies of our experience, including, if Johnson is correct, that monument to human creativity, the city. Look at any map, and it is apparent that cities form the nodal points of the human experience, where knowledge, information, goods, and services interchange. Cities have been with us so long that it is almost impossible to imagine life without them. There was, however, a time when they were not. Yet if we had never had cities, it is not immediately obvious why we would have needed them. Life in the countryside seems just fine, far from the maddening crowd and all those other things so complained about by those who visit and inhabit the cities of our planet. Yet cities happen and, perhaps more remarkably, they endure over time, indeed a very long time and with amazing consistency in terms of who lives where, and what they do. New York has its Garment District, Venice its goldsmiths, and both have been doing business in the same location for years—in the case of Venice, perhaps a thousand years. So why are there cities, and why do they look and feel as they do?

To be sure there are some cities whose existence and shape was a matter of plan. Somebody woke up one morning and said, let's build Washington, D.C. USA, Canberra, Australia or Brasilia, Brazil, and because these were all seats of government their formation and layout was due in no small part to the needs of government. A place for the legislature, embassies, executive offices—planned and managed civil construction, to be sure. But once built, such cities often (always) lack a certain something. People complain about the sterility of the official buildings, and so the city planners, in order to be obliging, plan neighborhoods, which unfortunately, look planned, and not like neighborhoods.

If Johnson, reporting the work of Jane Jacobs, is correct, the creation of most cities, and the "humanization" of all cities has little to do with planning. It seems to happen all by itself following certain very simple principles or preconditions. The mediating mechanism is nothing more glorious than the common sidewalk. "In the popular democracy of neighborhood formation, we vote with our feet."[22]

---

[22] *Op cit* pg 91.

AND THE BIG QUESTION: WHEN DO WE EAT?

For the countless millions inhabiting the cities of the earth, a major question regularly arises, typically three times a day. When do we eat? And surprisingly enough, for most people, most of the time, the answer is re-assuring. Whenever you want. Please understand I am by no means unaware of (or comfortable with) the obvious inequities present in our world, but I do think it is remarkable that the feeding system of the planet works as well as it does. And even more remarkable, nobody planned it. To make this point, particularly when dealing with systems thinking graduate students, I pose a problem, or more exactly, suggest an exercise. Starting out with praise for their understanding and application of the principles of systemic thinking, I ask that they put it all to work. Please design a system, I say, which will have the following characteristics: It will feed 8 million people everyday, just about anything they want, whenever they want it, and always have two weeks food supply on hand. When I see that they are in a real lather, either because they believe they have a solution close at hand, or know that they will never achieve one, I break in with a smile. Sorry to interrupt, but actually this was sort of a joke. You don't have to work so hard, because the system has already been built. It is called New York City.

Of course, you could substitute the name of any major city in the world—or small village, for that matter—and the point would be the same. The complex organization which feeds us every day (barring certain lapses) happened all by itself. Nobody organized it. Nobody manages it, although many people try. The Public Health Departments of the world do their best to insure that the available food is non-poisonous. And the restaurant critics in the press alert us to delights to be sampled, as well as those to be avoided. But at the end of the day, and on every day, the system does it all by itself.

Occasionally, some people think they have a better idea, and our recent experience with the so called "managed economy" of the Soviet Union is a painful case in point. The ideals were glorious, and the perception of the problems of an impoverished population painfully accurate. The actual execution, however, seemed to be more than a little flawed. Under the watchful eye of the state it seemed that the incredible complex adaptive system devoted to the feeding of the population came quite close to withering away. Visitors to the Soviet Union will attest to the fact that unless you were incredibly fortunate (due to luck or political position), getting a good meal, well served, was nearly impossible. Towards the end, the lack of good meals and good service were the least of the problems. Failing the influx of massive amounts of grain from the West, starvation was a genuine possibility.

This critique of the Soviet Union, particularly when offered by an American, could be taken as an ideological dispute, pitting Capitalism against Communism. My point is much more basic, even mundane. We are working much too hard creating and sustaining (managing) something which seems to do pretty well all by itself.

WHAT COMPLEX ADAPTIVE SYSTEMS DO

We now come to the heart of the matter with the question, what do Complex Adaptive Systems do? The short answer: They muddle through. Given the elegance of the science involved, and the polished erudition of those who record its progress, *muddling through* appears disappointingly mundane. And that is exactly the point. It is mundane, an every day occurrence for all of the 14 billion years that there have been days. Mind boggling complexity, monstrous diversity, massive chaos, are all tossed into the pot, creating the cosmic stew which is our home. Just an ordinary day's work in the Universe.

One could ask, however, how it could be that the fact that it is mundane comes as such a surprise. And the answer, I think is that for most people, most of the time, there is no surprise. It is only the relative few (largely in the West) who, having arrived at the exalted level of consciousness which I called Intellect, and inhabiting organizations I have called Proactive, who understand that order and systems can only be the product of our effort. If we didn't do it, it simply couldn't have happened. After all, somebody must be in charge. All of the rest of the world has a considerably more humble view of our role in the ordering of things. And so for them, what we perceive as impossible, they perceive to be obvious. It may be past time for us to be struck by a blinding flash of the obvious.

Despite our disbelief, even abhorrence, I think it fair to say that there is massive good news in the workings of the mundane engine of Muddling Through, The Complex Adaptive System, especially as we approach the awesome task of Peacemaking. For Peace to occur (and continue) which simultaneously includes and transcends chaos, confusion and conflict, we now know, or at least should know, that it cannot come about in pieces. Step by step won't make it. One bite at a time insures that when the meal is over, we will not be around to enjoy it. We may practice systemic analysis and multi-factorial development with abandon, but no matter the elegance of our analysis or the energy of our strategies, the butterfly will always show up, the mega-monster of complex diversity, which is our common humanity, will blow our plans away. In short, we do not have the horsepower. But the everyday, mundane, run of the mill, purely average, Complex Adaptive System, has chaos, complexity and diversity for lunch, and begs for more. If it is horsepower we need, it is just sitting there and waiting for us. At least that is a story worthy of pursuit, I believe.

THE OPEN SPACE EXPERIMENT

To this point I have, of necessity, relied on the work of others in order to paint a picture of the emerging consensus regarding self-organization and its potential for building our understanding of our selves, our world, and most importantly, the critical task of Peacemaking. Needless to say, I have only touched the tip of the iceberg, so to speak. I hope I have done so with some degree of fidelity, but if you are looking for the definitive treatment, this is not the place, and I am definitely a secondary source. However, the experience and emerging conclusions of others, previously described, correlates very closely with the results to date on an ongoing, natural experiment with which I have been closely associated since its inception. Open Space Technology has been used thousands of times, all over the world, with virtually every imaginable sort of group and situation. The results have been consistent, and may therefore be a useful addition to the general understanding of self-organization as it might apply to the human side of things. Of equal importance, Open Space Technology may also be understood as a bridge between a general understanding of self-organization, and its application to the concrete, and critical, issues of Peacemaking.

In 1985, when I first designed Open Space Technology (OST), it is fair to say that I didn't have a clue what I was really doing. OST emerged more as an intuition than as a carefully crafted methodology, and while it is certainly true that retrospectively it is clear that many strands of my life and experience, to say nothing of the hard work of others, played a major part in the creation, at the moment it was all need and luck.

The need derived from the fact that I had committed to host a gathering of peers and colleagues all concerned with the emerging field of Organization Transformation. We had met several times previously, and I had actually convened the first engagement. Both previous conferences had been put together in very much the traditional mode with speakers, panels, and small group discussions. In order to launch the first one, I devoted the better part of a year to the effort, bringing all the constituent elements of people, place and subject matter together. I assumed that is the way such things had to be done, but when the great day arrived and the conference convened, it was clear to me, and I think many others, that the truly useful, inspiring, and exciting parts occurred mostly in the coffee breaks. All the rest appeared, to some large extent, as wasted effort. As I approached the task of organizing the third gathering it was clear to me that no matter what I might do, it could not be what I had done before. I did not have the time, resources or energy.

I did, however, have two martinis while sitting on my patio enjoying the early spring weather of Washington and contemplating the up coming conference. The first martini enabled me to go beyond the shocking recognition that a full year's effort at conference organization had only resulted in the creation of interruptions to what turned out to be the main event: The Coffee Break. With the second martini, I found myself reflecting on those times in my experience when it seemed that people productively got together with ease and elegance to deal with major issues, without the benefit of planning committees, or an army of facilitators and meeting managers. The image that came to mind was the village assemblies I had witnessed in a small Kpelle village in West Africa. The significant piece, it seemed to me, was that they always gathered in a circle. And that turned out to be the first part of Open Space. Gather in a circle.

Substantive discussion, however, requires that people have some idea of what they need to talk about. In place of the standard agenda setting committee, I thought about a bulletin board. All over the world, when people have something of importance to communicate, they post it on a bulletin board, in one way or another. And that was the second part of Open Space. Create a bulletin board.

Having assembled, and now with the pertinent issues identified, it remains only to handle the practicalities of who, where, what, and when. The image that came to my mind at that point was of an indigenous market place. These natural wonders of human intercourse just seem to pop up like mushrooms all over the world. Unlike mushrooms, these markets can endure for centuries, convening at the same time and place, year in and out. And the most remarkable thing is that nobody seems to be in charge. To be sure, many people try, but buyers and sellers follow their own drummers. And if one way of organization doesn't work, a new one appears. And that was the final piece of OST, open a market place.

At that moment, the martinis ran out, and I felt comfortable that I had done all I could do. Several months later, some 85 brave souls gathered in a circle, created a bulletin board, opened a market place, and got on with the business at hand. And much to the surprise of everybody, it all worked. A three day symposium had been organized in something less than 12 hours, complete with topics, sessions, conveners, and participants. No hassle, no fuss, no bother. Just do it.

For 5 years our annual gathering happened in Open Space. During that 5 year period I considered Open Space to be an "interesting thing" we did, but having no broader application, or interest. Along about 1990 Open Space escaped, as it were, into the larger community, and all the rest is history. And it has been a fairly remarkable history—which nobody has ever bothered to carefully document, if only because the vast majority of those involved were infinitely more concerned with "doing" as opposed to keeping exact records and writing papers. As a guess, Open Space has been used perhaps 20–30 thousand times in 80 countries around the world, with groups ranging in size from 5–2000 participants. The presenting issues have included such things as Peace in the Middle East, creating the AT&T Pavilion for the 1996 Olympics, building roads on Native American lands, and many, many more. The number of Open Space practitioners (those who facilitate Open Space often, or occasionally) would probably number 10,000.

The numbers are an educated guess at best, but whatever the numbers, it is definitely clear that the Beta Tests have long since been completed. Open Space Technology, as an approach to productive, efficient, and effective meetings, is no longer a new, radical approach. It appears, at very high levels of probability, that when groups of people convene around an issue of genuine concern, sit in a circle, create a bulletin board, and open a market place; they will get on with the business.

OPEN SPACE AS A NATURAL EXPERIMENT

From 1990 until the present moment, the worldwide spread of Open Space and the continuing demonstration of its effectiveness has created a most interesting question: Why does it work? Until that fateful day when my two martinis did their work, it is safe to say that there was nothing in my conscious experience, or in the organizational literature with which I was familiar, that would suggest that inviting people to sit in a circle, create a bulletin board, and open a market place would produce anything other than massive confusion. I knew by virtue of my training, and prior experience, that in order to create order, you had to organize. And organization required endless attention to detail, finely tuned models, rigorous management, and enormous effort. The experience in Open Space had to be an aberration, for nothing in the theory or practice of management, as I knew it, would predict, or even allow, that experience to occur. At the very least it was improbable—possibly illegal, immoral and fattening! Definitely wrong. But it happened. Not once, but thousands of times. And so the inevitable question. Why?

Clues to the answer to this question had actually been arriving on my intellectual doorstep for some time, given my fascination with the phenomenon of self-organizing systems, but it was not until I read Stuart Kauffman's *At Home in the Universe* that the great A-ha experience broke through. Specifically, I was struck by the similarity between Kauffman's preconditions for self-organization (safe nutrient environment, diversity, complexity, etc.) and my own conditions for the use of Open Space. When asked the obvious and necessary question about when Open Space would be effective, my typical response was as follows. Open Space works and works well, in any situation characterized by the following: 1) A genuine issue of mutual concern which elicits a high degree of passion. 2) High levels of complexity in terms of the elements of the issue. 3) High levels of diversity in terms of the people involved. 4) The presence of actual or potential conflict. 5) A decision time of yesterday; in short the issue was a not a sometime thing, but demanded immediate attention. In another place[23] I have attempted a more detailed comparison, but for present purposes it is probably sufficient to offer my conclusions. Open Space works because self-organization works. Further, my conditions for use were (quite serendipitously) Kauffman's preconditions for self-organization. I believe we are talking about the same thing.

There has been, and probably will continue to be, debate around whether or not Open Space really is self-organization at work. I welcome the debate, if only because I think it will bring greater clarity to our understanding of self-organization, and also Open Space. But while the debate continues, I feel comfortable with my conclusions all of which fall under the heading of, "If it walks like a duck, quacks like a duck, and looks like a duck, there is a high degree of probability that it is a duck." Not high science perhaps, but if Open Space is not self-organization at work, it is clearly the next best thing.

More importantly, I find that the evolving theory of self-organizing systems as described by the folks cited to this point, and many more not mentioned, is the only thing that enables me to make sense of Open Space. According to the more conventional theory of organization, Open Space can't happen. According to my understanding of the evolving theory of self-organizing systems, what happens in Open Space is predictable. Call it as you will, but the equation of self-organization and Open Space works for me.

---

[23] *The Power of Spirit: How Organizations Transform,* Berrett-Koehler, 2000, pg 51.

Learning from Open Space

Presuming I am correct that Open Space Technology exemplifies self-organizing systems, the ongoing natural experiment with Open Space around the world has provided a depth of learning in two critical areas. First, we have come to understand the gifts of self-organization relative to the effective (and I would add *peaceful*) function of human communities. Second, we have learned much about what can be done, and not done, in order to initiate and sustain the process of self-organization. When it comes to utilizing the power of self-organization for the purposes of Peacemaking, such understanding is vital.

The gifts of self-organization, at least the sort of self-organization that takes place in Open Space, are multiple and useful. First of all there is the very practical gift of time and energy returned. Because the organization of a gathering is essentially done in the moment (usually in an hour or less) no matter the size of the group or complexity/conflict of the issue, all of the endless agenda setting meetings and process development planning sessions are eliminated. With the exception of basic logistics (a place, food, communications, travel, etc) what used to take a year can now be accomplished in less than an hour. Whew!

A second gift, no less valuable, is an exponential jump in the efficiency and effectiveness of the group and its work. Stories abound concerning projects that took 10 months being accomplished in 2 days, with final results that were as good or better. For example, the AT&T design team that was charged with the creation of that corporation's 1996 Olympic pavilion had taken 10 months to perfect their product. Then the situation shifted massively, and the original design was rendered useless. Worse yet, the Olympics were only 6 months away, and the building still had to be constructed. The 23 member design team met in Open Space, and in two days flat they had designed a totally new building, down to the level of working architectural drawings (not pretty, but functional) which all agreed was a major improvement aesthetically over its predecessor. My math is a little rusty, but 10 months (300 days) relative to 2 days appears to be something like a 1500 % increase in productivity. Obviously not every Open Space shows jumps like that, if only because not every Open Space deals with issues having such neat "before and after" measures. But what happened to AT&T is by no means an anomaly. And of course, the manifest power lies not in the magic of Open Space (or the mystery of two martinis). It is simply the awesome energy released when an everyday, ordinary, complex adaptive system gets to work.

Perhaps more impressive, although definitely less tangible in terms of objective measures, are what might be described as the "softer" gifts of Open Space, and similarly (I believe) the normative attributes of a well functioning self-organizing system. Every Open Space that I have participated in, and all that I have ever heard about, have shared the following behaviors and characteristics:

1) High Learning

2) High Play

3) Appropriate Structure and Controls

4) Genuine Community

High Learning is a modification of a phrase borrowed from Thomas Kuhn. Kuhn actually talks about High Science, those moments in the journey of scientific inquiry when paradigms are bent and busted, allowing new ones to appear. They are exciting, painful and productive. I have changed "science" to "learning" simply to make the point that you do not have to be an Einstein to participate, but the impact on the groups involved, if not the larger human community, is just as profound. Out of the chaos, confusion and conflict that typifies any good Open Space at the start, new ways of thinking and being together emerge. Antagonists find common ground. Opposing ideas and ideals clash and then synthesize into new and more powerful realities. The group finds itself in places it had never been before, never even thought about before. Needless to say this does not occur instantaneously or without fail, but it happens with sufficient frequency not to be surprising, although of course it is always a surprise to those involved.

High Play The quality of High Play is not trivial. In fact, play of all sorts, and High Play in particular, is very serious business, especially when people are engaged in the activity of generating and refining new ways of thinking together. As new realities are experienced and new maps or modes of thinking about them created—which is exactly what happens in Open Space when the High Learning begins—a playful atmosphere is essential, for play is the critical antidote to premature dogmatic attachment to any particular way of thinking.

When breakthroughs in thinking and acting occur, they do not come in neat packages. The edges are rough and there are lots of holes. As a consequence, gaining clarity on the new meaning is not usually a straight line affair. There is lots of backing and filling, rearrangement, and reformulation. All of which means that premature closure is deadly. And a premature attachment to "the right" way of looking at things will be disastrous. Here is where High Play makes its contribution, for by playing with ideas and manners of expression one has as much fun tearing things down as putting them together (and fun is important). Even though the thoughts and the issues may be heavy, a little lightness is in order.

Appropriate Structure and Controls It is sometimes suggested that in an Open Space environment, and by extension, in a self-organizing environment, structure and controls are somehow absent. Nothing could be further from the truth. Indeed both structure and controls are very much in evidence, often at a level of complex intricacy that would be the envy of any organizational design team. But the operative word is "appropriate." All structures and controls are emergent, built by the self-organizing system itself, and in the case of an Open Space, by the people involved. But their shape and form is usually a constantly changing phenomenon, for they are always appropriate to the task at hand, the people involved, and the environment in which everything is taking place. Change any one of these three (task, people or environment) and almost instantly new structures and controls emerge.

Genuine Community One of the most surprising characteristics of every Open Space I have ever been a part of is the appearance of what I can only call Genuine Community. This is to be distinguished from the sort of pseudo-community that appears all too often in our organizations when the CEO announces at the annual Christmas party that, "We are all one family." Or in the diplomatic world where phrases like the *Family of Nations* are bruited about. In both of those cases, one is tempted to smile—or more probably smirk—for seeing any relationship between "family" and "community," and the scene at hand would be a stretch. And yet, time and again in an Open Space, outright enemies come to respect each other. Real listening and real hearing occur more often than not. And towards the end of a gathering, it is not uncommon to see real hugs taking place, and even a few tears. The community manifested in Open Space is not of an idealized sort. Chaos, confusion and conflict abound. They are not avoided or suppressed, but transcended in the most remarkable way. Chaos seems to open space for new ideas, confusion clears the mind of old ideas, and conflict sharpens these new ideas and provides the basis for clear thinking and appropriate action. I would call it peaceful, but it is a very dynamic sort of Peace. Just the kind I think we desperately need.

The appearance of community in Open Space seems to occur automatically. There are no community building exercises, in fact the word "community" is rarely mentioned. Why this happens is a matter of some perplexity, but I think the other characteristics set the stage. When a group of people is immersed in High Learning, done in the spirit of High Play, differences (of opinion, background, culture) are appreciated and collectively form the creative environment out of which new ideas appear. Add in a strong dose of structure and controls which are all appropriate to the people, task and environment, and there would seem to be little to keep people apart. In a way you just can't avoid community, which is probably why it appears to break out naturally, and with little fanfare.

I suppose it would be gratifying if Open Space (my discovery) were to turn out to be the magic carpet carrying everybody to real community. I do not think, however, that the appearance of community has anything to do with the special magic of Open Space, or rather it has everything to do with the normal, natural function of a self-organizing system as it seeks to adapt itself to its environment. The search for fitness also requires internal fitness, or as I might prefer to say, wholeness, health and harmony amongst the constituent elements. *Simply put, the process of self-organization may be seen as a prime example of genuine Peacemaking. And it happens all by itself.*

And so a conclusion—or perhaps a desperate hope: *The power of self-organization energizes the deep processes of transformation. From the moment of the Big Bang until this present instant, we and the whole Cosmos have been led on the path towards genuine community. It is our search for fitness with ourselves and with our environment. It is the way of Peace—as wholeness, health and harmony—and it happens all by itself.*

With this conclusion, come two questions. If Peace happens all by itself, why are we in such a mess? And further, How do we deal with the pain? It is all very well to describe the journey of our lives in terms of a deep natural process which drives towards Peace, but along the way there are some very painful bumps.

CHAPTER V

The Pathology of Control and The Power of Grief-work

Putting the power of self-organization to work in the service of Peace appears more easily said than done, particularly when the whole process seems counter-intuitive to many, and simply invisible to more. And, should it turn out to be true, as I suggested at the conclusion of the previous chapter, that the creation of Peace is a natural concomitant function of any self-organizing system that occurs pretty much all by itself, why are we in such a mess, and how do we deal with the pain?

I believe there are two factors in play. The first is the self-inflicted injury which occurs when we pursue the phantom of Control. When life becomes tumultuous it is natural that we seek to gain control. But it seems that the harder we try the worse things become. I suggest that it is not that we are doing something wrong, rather that applying more control is the wrong response. This has nothing to do with giving up, but it has everything to do with letting go.

The second element in play is not self inflicted, unless we choose to make it so. If we are correct in our understanding of the process of self-organization, the forces of chaos, confusion and conflict play an essential and natural part, and without them the process would cease, indeed life would cease. It is also true that all three of these forces have decidedly unpleasant side effects, particularly when they appear at intense levels. It is understandable that we should attempt to limit, or eliminate, these effects, but when we are successful (and we never really are), the end result is often worse than the prior condition. It would appear that chaos, confusion and conflict come with the territory and are eliminated at our peril. The question then becomes, how do we survive the journey, or even better, thrive while on that journey?

There is a way which is essentially "hardwired" into each and every one of us. Formally known as Griefwork, it is the natural mechanism through which we handle the toxins of life. Just as in our biological lives, the metabolic process produces wastes which are eliminated by our plumbing system (Kidneys and excretory system), so also the waste products of self-organization (fragmentation, dis-ease, and dissonance) are removed by Griefwork. Life continues and thrives so long as both systems, plumbing and Griefwork, are in good repair. Life becomes difficult or impossible when these systems break down, which is often the result of our misguided efforts to redesign or control them. Truth to tell, both systems have been in operation for millions of years. They are very good at what they do, and we would be well advised to heed the adage "Don't fix it if it ain't broke." At least that is my belief which we will explore in this chapter.

THE PATHOLOGY OF CONTROL

It appears as an uncomfortable truth that the greater the effort devoted to controlling the surprises of life, large and small, the more it seems that things get out of control. Sooner or later, the best laid plans unravel. And more often than not, the resulting state is worse than the former one. In part this is the ongoing saga of unintended consequences. Flooding rivers are controlled with dikes and dams, and then the "Big One" comes and Mother Nature reminds us of our limited powers. Forest fires are extinguished only to leave mounds of tinder, which sooner or later ignite in massive holocausts. But more is at stake here than unintended consequences. Our efforts at control strike deeply at the very thing they were designed to protect, life itself. As we seek safety by consigning the restless movement of our lives to small containers and compartments which supposedly shield us from the potential adverse effects, life runs out of space and dies.

Our continuing experience with Open Space Technology is instructive. In a curious way, Open Space almost always seems to work, at least at a formal level. When people who are passionately concerned with a common issue gather in a circle, create a bulletin board, and open a market place, in very short order, they are ready for business. And more usually, already hard at work before any of the participants become fully aware of how much they have accomplished, or how easy it was.

There are a few times, however, when Open Space struggles, and sometimes just closes down. The obvious question is, what's the catch? Seventeen years of working with Open Space tells us it is just one thing: Control, the need to be in control and the attempt to exercise control. In fact we strongly advise people never to use Open Space if they have that need or even worse, actually think they are in charge. When the control button is pushed, the good work happening in Open Space shudders and may even stop, although more usually, the would-be controller is pushed to one side, gently, or with vigor, all of which attests to the power of self-organization despite our best efforts to control and organize it.

The lesson for me is a clear one. External, and usually arbitrary, control is the enemy of Open Space. When the Boss stands up and bellows, "I am in charge, and you will do what I say!" a beautifully occurring natural process experiences real difficulty.

Perhaps it is an unwarranted leap, but I would argue by extension that the mess we experience in our all too nonpeaceful world has, at least in part, a similar etiology. It is all those bosses, and "wannabe" bosses, struggling for control and seeking to impose their notion of how things ought to be done, that gets us in the pickle we find ourselves. Some may call their efforts leadership, but if so it is a very destructive force, upsetting the natural process and often preventing the very thing many of these world bosses say they are in favor of, Peace.

Over the course of our history, and fortunately more than occasionally, we have experienced a very different sort of leadership which accomplishes incredible things often in a most counterintuitive fashion. I think of Mahatma Gandhi, for one, who described (somewhat facetiously, I am sure) the function of the leader as determining the direction of the parade and racing to the front. Obviously there is more, and he did more, but one thing he clearly understood was the limitations of his own power to control. Instead he listened attentively to the ebb and flow of the emergent, self-organizing system which became his movement, and with surprising gentleness (non-violence), urged it along the path chosen, not by him, but by the people themselves. In the face of the enormous power of the British Empire, and all those who conspired with it, Gandhi accomplished what many choose to describe as a miracle. For myself, I see it as a natural occurrence which Gandhi had both the patience and sensitivity to nurture into fulfillment. I think it is possible for all of us to assume the role he chose for himself, and then to do what he did, no longer the exceptional performance of a saint, but an every day practice by common people, The Practice of Peace. This is not about giving up, as indeed Gandhi never gave up. It is all about letting go of the persistent delusion of control. We never had it; we will never get it. And to the extent that we try, we will succeed only in compounding our misery.

It is sometimes assumed, mistakenly I think, that letting go requires the avoidance of anything that might look like assertive behavior, and yet in the case of Gandhi it is absolutely clear that he rarely, if ever, flinched from taking a stand. The critical issue is not the absence of assertive behavior, but rather the manner in which it is used, and the individual's understanding of his or her actual role in the universe. When assertive behavior is exercised from the point of view that the agent is the lord of the universe, rather like the French king who proclaimed, "L'etat, c'est moi." (The state is me), it might seem that he was definitely in charge, yet the truth of the matter is that no single human being can possibly comprehend the mind-boggling, diverse complexity which is our world. Therefore any action, even well intended ones, are always blind sided and ill informed.

There is another way, which I think Gandhi superbly epitomized. It involves opening oneself (opening space) to the full spectrum of forces and possibilities, all the while understanding that they can never be fully understood, and then allowing the powers of intuition to guide one along pathways that are congruent with the flow of life. From such a place, meaningful, productive and assertive behavior can occur. Not always, not perfectly, but the probabilities rise dramatically.

This is not about the rejection of reason, but rather the transcendence of reason, for our rational capacities, though awesome, are simply inadequate to the task. But what reason alone cannot accomplish, our subconscious may well achieve. And our subconscious, I think, is home to our intuition. You may ask whether this psychology is in line with the best findings of that science. Truthfully, I don't know. But I do know that when my rational powers run out of road, my good old subconscious and intuition take over—provided I open sufficient space for them to move around in, and then pay attention to what is being said.

If everything works as hoped, my meager energy and powers are leveraged by the massive flows of life, and my contribution, large or small, coalesces. Then again, my assertive efforts may become just a curious side eddy, spinning off into oblivion. All of which means that for my sanity, I must hold my expectations for specific outcomes very lightly, or better yet, let them all go. I believe this is the way of Gandhi. I know it works for me.

Now, are we out of the Woods?

Now we come to a most interesting question: should it happen that all "wanna-be" leaders of our world were miraculously transformed into latter day Gandhis, would we escape from the mess we are in? Unfortunately, I think the answer is No. The reason is a simple one, having to do with chaos, confusion and conflict. As this fateful trio does its work—chaos opening space for new life, confusion muddling made-up minds opening the way for new ideas, and conflict bringing results in pursuit of full life—there are, unfortunately, unpleasant side effects which can, and often do, become toxic. Worse yet, they hurt. And the greatest hurt comes when things end, as they always do. How do we deal with the pain?

The Power of Griefwork

Somewhere, sometime, somehow you reach the end. The culprit may be time, money, your limitations as perceived by others, or by you, but you hit the wall. It may also be just the end. Like the wonderful one horse shay that fell apart all in a day, the end came for no particular reason, and the folks find themselves speeding towards a future they will never reach. They have simply run out of road.

This ending may come with the silence of exhaustion, like the conclusion of T.S. Eliot's "The Hollow Men," which acknowledges that "…this is the way the world ends, not with a bang, but a whimper." This was the experience of Eastern Airlines at the end of its corporate existence, after labor and management had battled each other to a standstill, fighting for a piece of the pie, which had already been eaten. There was no massive explosion, just the quiet shutting of doors. And two weeks later, hardly a sign could be found that the once mighty airline had ever existed.

The ending may equally be spectacular and cataclysmic, as when the powers of this world run out of patience, or see advantage, and choose to take the resolution of things into their own hands in the only way that seems possible at that moment. Forget about the moralities of the situation, the rights and wrongs, although each side will seek to present itself in its own perception of the best light, certain that God is on *their* side. The Allies strike Nazi Germany, Great Britain hits Argentina over the Falklands, Al Quaeda demolishes the Twin Towers and punches a large hole in the Pentagon, and the United States retaliates with all its might, making every attempt to reduce Afghan mountains to piles of rubble, and of course entombing such unfortunates that may be in the way. Rational arguments end and the situation is reduced to the lowest possible denominator of Darwinian evolution, kill or be killed, with the survival of the fittest.

No matter how it may come, or what the signs, when it is over, it is over. In all cases the tragedy is clear, the regrets inevitable. There should have been another way, good folks needn't have died or (as in the case of Eastern Airlines and other corporate endings) lost their livelihood. If only…But the "if onlies" do no good. They will not change a thing. It is over.

What is *not* over is the process of physical life itself. At least not yet. It may well seem to those caught in the fury of war's storms, or the silent desolation of a failed corporation, that life has suddenly gone out of control and rejected its fundamental principles. But viewed from the perspective of what we know about the 14 billion years of our collective cosmic history, life is not out of control, it is just being life. From the moment of the first Big Bang until the present instant, things have come and gone—sometimes with cataclysm, and sometimes in silence—but coming and going seem to be in the nature of things. It is a hard lesson, but an essential one. Life—the full continuum of life—from Quarks and other elemental particles up to, and including, *Homo sapiens,* was not created for our personal pleasure, comfort or continuance. Everything, it turns out, has a beginning, a middle, and an end. That is just the nature of things, and we are left with the inevitable question: How do we deal with the pain?

When the end comes, as it always does—whether caused by entropy or explosion—grief results. It begins with shock that turns to anger. Like the impact of an explosive wave hitting our chest, all the air is forced from our lungs. It is hard to breathe, maybe even impossible. The loss, the shame, the tragedy, the misery, all combine to create a monstrous emptiness in the center of our being. And breath—which is both the symbol and potentiator of life itself—appears to vanish. But only for a moment. Soon the void is filled with the inrush of the hot breath of anger. Blind anger, directed at anything and everything, but mostly at the perceived cause of ending. In war, the anger focuses on the enemy, those barbarous and cruel creatures that stripped life of its meaning, destroyed sons and daughters, family and friends. In corporate meltdown the anger is directed at greedy executives, selfish unions, avaricious investors. Anybody, everybody who conceivably had a part to play in the termination of what once seemed a rock of stability.

The anger also turns inward to our own inadequacies, imagined or real. All those things that we didn't do, and might have; the things we did, and shouldn't have. The inward anger creates guilt in the eddies of its passage. For a time, and it may be a long time, incoming waves of shock are answered by out flowing waves of anger.

In the moment it seems there are no other moments, for the shock and anger are all consuming. To the extent that thought and rational reflection exist, the thoughts are only of retribution, and we bask in the righteousness of our anger. Should it turn out that the agent of ending was some natural cataclysm, a flooding river or raging forest fire, the shock and anger are no less powerful, but the culprit is more elusive, which may leave us shaking our fists at the Universe and whatever power, or powers, occasioned our torment.

We are certain that nobody ever had such feelings and that our situation is unique, and of course it is unique, for nobody has ever been us. What is also true is that shock and anger at the moment of ending come just as naturally as hunger in the absence of food, or desire in the absence of sex. With the arrival of shock and anger we stand at the headwaters of one of the great flowing processes of life, a river that many have passed down before, and all will navigate sooner or later. It has been called Griefwork.

First described, I believe, by Elizabeth Kübler-Ross[24] and her colleagues, Griefwork has been with us since before we could remember, or record our memories. The rituals of death, practiced by ancient shamans and modern priests, acknowledge its presence, and assist its passage. Kübler-Ross's unique contribution was to recognize the elements of the process, and define the stages not only as an exercise in scientific discovery, but for very practical and therapeutic purposes. By knowing and understanding the stages it becomes possible to positively assist those who are on the journey, just as the midwife's knowledge of the stages of birth enables her to support the mother in labor. None of the stages can be skipped, for all are essential and contributory. Griefwork, like labor, is something you can only go through, and not around. And like labor, there is a purpose in the unpleasant process. A new child, in the case of labor, and new, or renewed, life out of the Griefwork. Grief may appear as a great pain, but it is also work in the sense of the primary definition of the word, an *activity in which one exerts strength or faculties to do or perform something.*[25]

In the early 80's it occurred to me that what Kübler-Ross described primarily in terms of an individual's process could apply equally well to the experience of a group, even very large groups, such as corporations and other organizations, in the midst of endings. Further, that with knowledge of this process, one could help them complete their journey. Experience of the past 20 years has brought that notion from theoretical speculation to a central part of my practice. Who

---

[24] Kübler-Ross, Elizabeth, *On Death and Dying,* Macmillan Paperback, 1970.

[25] Merriam-Webster's Collegiate Dictionary, 2000.

knows whether the theory is true, but I do know it works in the sense that it is predictive and productive.[26]

As I became increasingly fascinated with the phenomena of self-organizing systems, particularly as they seemingly play out at the level of human systems in general, and in the Open Space event in particular, I first suspected, and have now concluded, that Griefwork plays a special and essential part. I believe that Griefwork is the critical element which enables human systems to negotiate the journey through chaos on to new and higher levels of complexity, a journey which lies at the heart of our experience of self-organization. You will find the details in my last book.[27]

THE STAGES OF GRIEFWORK

When endings come for human beings, Griefwork starts. It is quite automatic, and will proceed to some conclusion all by itself. At one level, there is nothing to be done, for like breathing, the beating of the heart, and the progress of the gastrointestinal system, everything normally takes place without our will or intent. Also like these systems, there are occasions where a little assistance can be helpful. That is the function of the Peacemaker.

The process of Griefwork has been studied extensively and although the identified phases and their names may vary with the researchers, there appears to be a strong consensus, even in terms of the specifics. My version is based largely on the work of Kübler-Ross with some modifications and additions

---

[26] I have documented my thoughts and practice in two of my books, *Spirit: Transformation and Development in Organizations,* 1985, and in *The Spirit of Leadership,* Berrett-Koehler, 1999. The latter book had appeared in an earlier version with the title, *Leadership Is,* Abbott Publishing, 1990.

[27] *The Power of Spirit: How Organizations Transform,* Berrett-Koehler, 2000.

occasioned by my experience that the self-same process occurs with groups, as well as individuals. The stages I've identified are as follows:

1) Shock and Anger

2) Denial

3) Memories

4) Open Space as Despair

5) Open Space as Silence

6) Vision and Renewal

Shock and Anger

We have already described the initiating phase of the process, and adding more detail may be gratuitous. However we have not indicated what the positive attributes and contributions of this phase might be. For this phase, as all the phases, provides some necessary and critical element to the process, which means among other things, that avoiding the phase is to halt the operation.

Shock and anger is the essential first step in the process of healing for both the individual and the organization. Seen from the inside, it is all rage and pain. From the outside, it may appear terrifying and sometimes comic. The anger is genuine and when brought to bear in the fragile environs of our world, the results can be disastrous. The comic side appears when those caught in the anger seem for all the world like three year old children having a temper tantrum. But no matter the external appearance, the act itself is of critical importance. It enables the patient to breath. The positive contribution is almost purely physiological, and counters a potentially lethal side effect of shock.

When great insult overwhelms us, physically, psychologically, or both, we suck in our breath and hold it. The shoulders pull in, and it is not uncommon to see the face turn blue. Breathing, of course is essential to life, and restoring the process as quickly as possible is advisable. Anger does the trick. The scenario can take many forms, but the classic one is as follows. Insult followed by two words, *Ohhhhh...Shit!* Of course this varies with the language spoken, but the result is the same. It is virtually impossible not to breathe while saying (or better yet screaming) *Ohhhhh...Shit!* Of course it may take several tries to get it right and regular, which explains why for situations of major insult, the *Oh Shits* can continue for some time.

For the onlooker, such explosive behavior can be frightening. At best it is socially unacceptable, at worst it may actually be very destructive. In either case, there is a natural inclination to bring the expression of anger to a halt as quickly as possible. This is a drastic error. It may be advisable to contain the reaction, and thereby avoid damage to self and others, but do not stop the process, for the shock and anger has a critical task to perform, keep the patient breathing. Obviously the stakes go up considerably as the numbers of those affected increase. One person saying *Oh Shit* is a social embarrassment. Millions doing the same thing create a rather different problem. But they must say it if life is to continue.

Under ordinary circumstances, the shock and anger phase eventually fades as its task is completed. There is no precise timetable, and it will be over when it is over. But it will never be over if it is aborted midstream, or never effectively allowed to begin. The result is that the people involved remain stuck in a most uncomfortable and unproductive place, continuing their state of shock and anger. I suspect that we have all seen tragic victims of such a fate. They begin and end every day in anger, which poisons their lives, and the lives of those around them.

Denial

The second step of the Griefwork process is Denial. For those in the area, who have not been immediately affected by the traumatic insult, the behavior of Denial can seem impossibly maddening, even boring. No matter the evidence, or the effort made in attempting to convince these people to the contrary, they continue to act as if "it" had never happened. They may even be able to verbalize that the ending has taken place, but the old patterns continue. They get dressed for a job that no longer exists. They set a place at the table for someone who no longer eats. They endlessly debate the politics of a nation state that has passed away. In the face of such behaviors it is almost impossible to avoid expressing exasperation in words like: "It's over. Get on with your future. Stop crying over spilt milk. Face reality." But, here is the point, they are facing a reality that hurts too much.

Denial is very much like a bandage on a major wound, providing protection until it heals, or like morphine to dull the pain. When the healing begins, and the pain subsides neither bandage nor morphine are needed. But until that time, the pain of ending is such that no life is possible, or if possible, then not bearable, without their protection. Forcibly tearing away the protective cover of Denial would be like ripping off a bandage from a fresh wound. In a moment all the pain returns, and we are back to where we started, or worse.

Denial, like shock and anger, may be aborted, but not without damage. Just as people can remain stuck in their shock and anger, so also denial, and until the process has run its course, such "stuckness" is the likely outcome. And we all know people who have gotten stuck, living each day as if nothing had changed, avoiding any and all clues of the passage. And the more obvious and inescapable the clues of passage become, the deeper these folks hide in their Denial, until hardly a thing remains to tell us that somebody is home. By and large, they are quite harmless, unlike their perpetually angered counterparts, but no less tragic. Denial is necessary; it must run its course and give its gift. Only then will life move one.

Memories

The third step in the Griefwork process, as I have come to understand it, is Memories. At a superficial level this stage sounds much like its predecessor but there is a distinct difference in tone, if not in substance. The major focus continues to be on the past—all the things that happened, might have happened, should have happened—but with a difference. It is now painfully clear to everybody involved that the end did in fact come. What was no longer is. And so the memories. Some bitter, some sweet, all important.

In Memories, there is an enormous amount of story telling, which is of course the age old way we recall and share our memories. In most cases, the story telling occurs in informal settings when folks gather for work or play, and in the quiet spaces. You hear the words, "Do you remember when…?" And out comes the tale. At first hearing, it all seems quite random and happenstance. Some present occurrence triggers a memory, and the tale is told.

After a while, a pattern becomes apparent. Some tales are told repeatedly with variations, again, and again, and again. These tend to be the core stories of heroes, heroines, and mighty acts. It is as if the community were reflecting on its heritage in preparation for whatever future lies ahead. And I think that is precisely what is happening. As each tale is told, the core value is raised to consciousness, considered in the light of the new, changed circumstances, and either filed away in the dusty archives, or given an enduring place in the collective memory. No committee meets, nor does the editorial board convene, but slowly and deliberately the collective consciousness makes its choices. This comes with us on the road to the future. This we sadly leave behind. It is the continuing process of self-definition and self-understanding occasioned by the end of the old, and the appearance of something new that is yet to be understood fully.

Telling the many tales also provides opportunity to honor the heroes and heroines, some of whom will not make it in the new reality, and more than a few may have already departed professionally, geographically, or even violently from this life itself. Telling these stories is a way of offering thanks for what has been done, and also gathering strength for what is to come. It is a way of cleaning the shop before departure.

It is also noteworthy that most of the stories seem to start, in one way or another, from the same point in time, The Moment When It Happened. Often introduced with the question, "Where were you when...?" In the United States, as my compatriots processed their grief following the assassination of John Kennedy, that question was heard over and over, and I never knew anybody who could not recall precisely where they were at the moment the news came through. Exactly the same thing happened after the tragedy of 9/11, and it continues, for that Griefwork has scarcely begun. In the U.K. during the days and weeks surrounding the death of Princess

Dianna, the British, quite uncharacteristically, talked incessantly about their personal answer to that question.

I cannot claim to have made a comprehensive study of the matter, but I do know that every place in the world where I have encountered significant moments of ending, the same question is asked, and the story is told. My interpretation is that by repetitively telling the several stories beginning from the moment of ending, and spreading out to include the events of the present moment, individuals and the whole community, are effectively retelling and reinterpreting their common story in the light of that particular shattering event. Once finished, although it never is completely, a new fabric of consciousness emerges which gives meaning to the critical event, and all the other events and actions of the common life.

There is a lot going on with all this story telling: Honoring heroes, letting go of unneeded baggage, weaving a new fabric of collective meaning preparatory to jumping off into an unknown, and unknowable, future. To outsiders, and that includes the Peacemakers if they are also outsiders, the tale quickly becomes an old one. But it needs to be told in order that the essential work of letting go and moving on may take place.

Open Space as Despair
Sooner or later the tale has been told sufficiently. There is nothing more to say and then what remains is silence. But it is not an easy silence, but rather a gaping hole in the fabric of life. An open space in which all the dreams, hopes, and plans of another time have disappeared. No longer blurred by the fury of Shock and Anger, masked by the balm of Denial, or celebrated and recalled in the time of Memories, there is just silence, emptiness, hopelessness.

Of all the pains that humanity experiences, I think Despair is the worst. It is born of the certain knowledge that what had been a central part of life, perhaps even life itself, is no more, and will never return. Smiling faces that used to warm the day are all veiled. Plans for a future, now destined never to arrive, are all in shreds. Rock solid certainties that guided behavior and made life meaningful, if not fun, have all dissolved. There is only Despair in the literal sense of the word, being without hope, hanging like a dark, wet fog over everything. It is the moment of the final letting go, for there is nothing left to hang on to, and we have come face to face with that reality.

Despair, like all other elements of Griefwork, has its gifts. Although in the moment those gifts hardly seem attractive. In Despair we come to appreciate fully how much we really loved that which we grieve—be that a way of life, place of work, a group of people, or an individual. It is an appreciation, unfortunately, that can never be fully realized until the object of our affection is torn from our grasp. However, it is only when we have deeply appreciated what we have lost that we can fully release our attachment. And with that release we become free for whatever might be coming next. It is only when the space of our lives is sufficiently open that we can truly welcome the new.

The pain of Despair only seems to increase over time, for the more we appreciate that which we've lost, the more painful the loss becomes. But in retrospect, when despair passes, which it eventually does for most of us, it becomes clear that the pain we experience is, to some large extent, self-inflicted. It is the pain of holding on to that which no longer exists. Once we let go, the pain departs. And the sooner we let go, the sooner the pain ends. The ultimate gift of Despair, therefore, is to provide us with some very strong motivation to get on with life.

I am a man, and therefore have had no personal experience with the process of birth, at least as a woman may experience it, but I am told that as the contractions of labor extend over time, they intensify in power and also in pain. Each succeeding contraction is more painful than its predecessor, and there is no going back. And the last one is typically the grand wizard of them all, but it is also the moment of birth. I experience Despair in much the same way. It is at once the darkest point in the whole journey of Griefwork, and the engine of breakthrough. There is no way to avoid it; one can only go through it. But once through it, there is release, and the result, much like the process of birth itself, is new life, or at least the potential for new life.

It may also be helpful to remember that as with all other stages of Grief, it is possible to get stuck. When Despair is avoided, we are condemned to live a life in despair. We know such people, and their tragedy is a double one. Not only have they lost something very precious, they live in perpetual agony over the loss. Somewhere, somehow, they never took the leap.

Open Space as Silence
On the other side of Despair is more open space, a lot more open space, but now manifested as silence. Not dead silence, but that pregnant silence when nothing and everything is present, but only as expectation. The old is now gone. The frenzy of Shock and Anger, the respite of Denial, the joy and sadness of Memories, and last but not least, the crucible of Despair have all done their work. It is definitely over, but the new, whatever the new might be, has yet to arrive. Caught between what was, and what shall be there is silence. Like

the instant between breathing in and breathing out, or that incredible moment before a baby's first breath, there is silence. It is the silence of ending and the possibility of beginning. The rich chords and discords of life have come to a point of resolution. Will the music stop, or find new voice?

I experience this moment as a holy moment. It is the moment of creation, or perhaps the moment before creation, when everything is a possibility, and nothing is there. For those who occupy such a moment—and we all do sometime or other—this is a moment of choosing. Do we go on, or stay? Cross the open space to whatever may lie ahead, or simply reside in that timeless silence?

There is, so far as I can see, no right choice or wrong choice, there is only our choice, and only we can make it. Should we choose to stay in that moment without time, I believe that choice must be respected.

Who knows why some choose to stay and some choose to go, but every time I have found myself in such a place, my choice to go forward was always occasioned by a question, What was I going to do with the rest of my life? And others, who have described their time in that place, seem to have responded to the same question. The means by which that question was asked are as various as the pathways of life itself. For some it is the rising of the sun on another day, suggesting that there are more days to follow. For others the question appears in the smile of a child, reminding us of a future that waits to be entered. And very often it is a question posed in the words of somebody who cares. What are you going to do for the rest of your life?

The question is important, but its mode of asking equally so. When that question is asked out of caring, or as I would prefer to say, Love—its power is incredible. Love, like Peace is one of those words with so many possible meanings that it becomes essential to say what you mean. For me, Love always has two faces, a face of acceptance, and a face of challenge. Love as *acceptance* takes us for what we are, as we are, and with no questions asked. Good, bad, or indifferent, we are OK.

But acceptance alone is not sufficient, although it is certainly comfortable. For if we are only loved for what we are, and not also for what we might become, there is the almost unavoidable temptation to grow flabby. By definition there are no standards against which we might measure ourselves. Such love quickly degenerates into pink foam. Pretty, but without substance.

Fortunately, there is another face to love, which I call *challenge*. This is the rigorous, no nonsense, expectation that we live up to our potential. Challenge becomes destructive when left to its own devices, as does acceptance. It becomes very destructive when attached to particular outcomes—perhaps becoming a lawyer when our potential was to be an artist.

When challenge and acceptance come together there is full, powerful love. And the greater the challenge, and the greater the acceptance, the greater the love. In such love we can be just the way we are, and strive to become everything we can be. At the critical moment when the question is asked, "What are you going to do for the rest of your life?"—, it is more than possible if it is asked with radical acceptance and radical challenge that the question will reach us and that we will respond. When the response comes, it may begin with three little words. *I wonder if…*I wonder if we can create a new country? I wonder if I may find a new job? I wonder if…? When wonder and imagination come together a marvelous new thing is born. It is called Vision. And with the arrival of Vision we come to the end of Griefwork, and the beginning of whatever is to happen next.

Vision

Vision is absolutely not to be confused with its contemporary profanation, The Vision Statement. Vision is never the product of a committee, still less the idle thinking of the CEO. And it certainly never appears in neat sentences with bullet points. Vision, at least when it first bursts upon the scene, is messy, wild and wonderful. It comes in all colors, shapes and sounds. Miles from rational argument, it sparkles with energy and spirit. Born in the furnace of Shock and Anger, protected by Denial, nurtured by Memories, purified in the crucible of Despair, and gestated in the womb of Silent Open Space, Visions often explode into being. From their power comes inspiration, which may then bring forth rational plans and effective actions. But Vision at its inceptions is not unlike the Big Bang which began it all—lots of heat, light and power.

Of course, it may turn out to be just another flash in the pan, lots of light and smoke, but no substance, but only time will tell. But in the moment, there is good news. Life has renewed itself. Once again the Complex Adaptive System is back in business.

OPEN SPACE RECONSIDERED

You may have found it curious that I have used the words *open space* in such various, and apparently dissimilar, ways. In the beginning it was all about a meeting methodology, and by the end, open space referred to a critical time/space in our human journey, the place of ending and beginning, the site of creation. I must confess that the words in my vocabulary were initially used in the latter context, for open space exclusively referred to that "holy time/space." At the time, Open Space Technology had not emerged from the spirit of two martinis, but when it did, I discovered something I believed to be quite remarkable, and very surprising. Every time we opened space in the sense that we sat in a circle, created a bulletin board, and opened a marketplace, it appeared that we (the whole group) entered into something that looked exactly like the Griefwork process I have been describing. This was particularly so in high stakes/high conflict situations. We typically began in chaos very much feeling the end of something vital. There was no small amount of Shock and Anger—bitching most people called it. Followed by Denial, lots of story telling (Memories) and often reaching that deathly quiet place of Despair. And then, more often than not, the space was crossed and we encountered the great energizer, Vision. And of course, the end was celebration, not because we planned a party, but because there was nothing else to do. If you look back over my stories of the Open Space in South Africa, and also the one with USWEST, I think you will see the footprints of Griefwork as they passed by. And when you do your next (or first) open space, as I dearly hope you will, I believe you will see the same thing. So when it came to naming our strange new approach to better meetings, Open Space seemed to be the only possibility.

THE MOVEMENT TOWARDS PEACE: GIFTS OF SELF-ORGANIZATION AND GRIEFWORK

Peace, as I have come to understand it, arises naturally in the ongoing process of self-organization as our world, and all of its multiple communities seek fitness with themselves and their environment manifested as wholeness, health and harmony.

Not without chaos, confusion, conflict, and death, which are all integral to a process which both includes and transcends them, because the realization of Peace can be painful. But it is a pain we can bear positively and productively as Grief does its work.

Peace, I think, is a natural condition which does not require the arrival of the Kingdom of God. The fundamental mechanisms are already present, and as we gain knowledge and experience, we, like Gandhi, can assist that process in very conscious, strategic, and tactical ways. My intention for the balance of this book is to suggest what some of these ways might be, relate some of my experiences to date, and open the space for your further contributions. I think we already know a great deal, certainly sufficient to make a good start. But our present knowledge and practice is minimal, both in terms of the need and the possibilities. So this is an invitation to go deeper.

It may of course be an invitation you would prefer to decline, if only because it could appear as a solicitation to join Don Quixote battling windmills. In the event that the rhetoric has passed all reasonable limits, a short story may serve to bring us back to earth.

OPENING SPACE FOR PEACE IN ROME

As I write, the killing in The Middle East continues and grows worse. The Israelis seek to control the situation by building yet more fences, creating more Check Points, sending out more soldiers, all in the name of restoring the Peace, or if not Peace, then at least some semblance of security. The results to date have not been promising. Raising the level of military presence seems only to inspire more violence. Some would argue that the Palestinian response is a calculated strategy, others would see it as an act of desperation, committed by people who are flat out of options. Either way, the daily statistics of suicide attacks and Israeli military counterattacks continue, and nobody can mistake the fact that security has not been achieved, and Peace is but a hope.

The odd part is that the "end game" is pretty clear to everybody, if not in detail, then certainly in outline. The catch phrase is, "Land for Peace." The Israelis return to the pre-1967 borders, the Palestinians become a separate state, and life should go on. But how to get to that end game? The way things are currently going shows little promise of getting where everybody, it seems, wants to go.

A growing group of people in Israel and Palestine have concluded that while military action may be inevitable at the moment, and that diplomatic activity is essential, neither by themselves, or both together, will be effective. The wounds are too deep, painful and old. Further military action only increases the severity of the wounds, and the would-be diplomats are locked in positions that provide scant space for reasonable and lasting solutions. Other, deeper work is required.

Specifically, the overall environment has to be improved such that the tensions that create armed thrust and counter thrust are reduced, and space is provided for the diplomats to do their job. It may sound like a very weak reed, but some honest, face to face, intense conversation amongst the antagonists might just start the process, and if that conversation can be continued and broadened, the needed environmental change may take place. Not exactly a new idea, but certainly with a new twist, for the intent is to start, or perhaps re-start the natural processes of self-organization so that the two complex adaptive systems known as Israel and Palestine can do what can only be done naturally—find Peace in themselves, and with each other.

It began in Rome with a most remarkable Open Space gathering. Truthfully, as an Open Space, it was in fact unremarkable. Things happened just about as our seventeen year experience tells us they would. What was different was that nobody, including myself, really thought it could work. We had hope for sure, but hope bordering on the thin edge of despair. My report, written two days after the event, follows.

Note: The Open Space described here took place in a villa in Rome, which seemed to be the closest neutral turf. The date was June 6–9, 2002. It was sponsored by the Italian Foreign Ministry, the Education for Life Foundation, and The Centro Dionysia. I had been asked to facilitate the gathering, and I have written this as my story, for after all it is the only one I can tell. The details of the discussion remain with the participants as they requested.

Fifty Palestinians and Israelis gathered in Rome to talk about themselves, their future, and the possibilities of Peace. They met in Open Space.

Two days before the opening of the gathering, yet another incident took place. I do not know the details, and they really don't matter, but in a moment the possibility of the convergence in Rome hung by a thread. The Israeli government moved on Ram Allah and only by very quick actions were the delegates from that city moved to Jerusalem a day early so that they could make the trip. Once in Rome, all 50 came to the Centro Dionsyia, a marvelous 500 year old villa which over looks the Basilica of St. Peter. We thought to meet in a large pavilion located in the gardens, but upon arrival the rains came too. Not just a little rain but sheets and torrents, dark clouds, high winds, thunder, lightening.

The dripping participants moved inside the villa for the opening ceremonies, but the time was late, and they were tired, some having been on their feet for 24 hours. So the opening remarks by the Italian minister for the Middle East were put to the side, as were the greetings from the conference organizers. We began with some powerful comments by Nada, a Serbian who has been working ceaselessly in that troubled part of the world. How to deal with your anger, pain and despair, all spoken from the heart and from experience. We ate and went to bed.

The next morning 50 Palestinians and Israelis sat in a circle under the pavilion. I opened the space asking each person to look around the circle and notice the people. It was quite a group. Not just your standard "peace-nics," but people from the right and the left politically and religiously.

I began by saying that I had come because I cared for my friends in Palestine and Israel, and also for myself and my children. And although the people in that circle may feel themselves isolated and alone in their own private Hell with their own agonizing story, that story was also the story of our world. Like it or not, they were in the hot crucible of the future of humankind. The future of all of us is being created in that strange place known as the Holy Land, even as it has been for millennia. So I cared, but I was also on the edge of despair or beyond. I could not think of any way out. The issues were so deep and intractable that movement appeared impossible. Space was closed. But still I came, and still I cared, as I presumed was true for each of them as well.

When the present is closed, and the future confused, sometimes the past can be helpful, and I recalled a time 10 years earlier when I happened to be in South Africa as Mandela was released from prison. We did an Open Space then in Capetown, and people sat in a circle fearing a future that appeared all too dark and bloody. Over the several years following Mandela's release, as I came and went, my friends in the US and Europe would ask me what I thought about the possibilities. To their surprise and mine too, I said I thought that South Africa would make it. Not without problems for sure, but they would make it. When asked why, I responded that there were two things I knew about every South African. They all loved their land with something approaching mystic intensity. And secondly, they all loved to sing. I felt that people who loved their land, and loved to sing, would find the way, as they seem to be doing.

I knew that each person sitting in that circle in Rome also loved their land. They too loved to sing. Maybe we would find a way. But that way would not be easy, having many dark and fearful places. But we could not avoid the dark, or we would never see the light. We had to go deep. Each one of us must make that journey by ourselves, but it always helps to have a friend. So I invited them to find a friend, best of all a new friend, and don't forget to sing. And so we started.

The open circle quickly filled with people announcing the issues they cared about passionately, and were prepared to take responsibility for their discussion, and hopefully, resolution. In 20 minutes flat, the work for the next two days was on the wall. It was not a pretty picture, and hard work in abundance lay ahead, but we were under way. All day long, in the usual way of Open Space, the conversation continued.

Sessions convened and dispersed. The details of those conversations are known only to the participants, but sitting in that space, I felt an incredible flow of passion and desire, hope and exasperation, fear and no small amount of trembling. It was all coming out. But as we came to the end of the day, there was a Peace which did not exclude chaos, confusion and conflict, but somehow transcended them all.

We gathered in the circle for Evening News. I had a branch from an olive tree for our talking stick.[28] And we shared. Fifty Palestinians and Israelis sitting in a circle, passing an olive branch each to the other.

The next morning broke clear. Not a cloud in the sky. The warm Italian Sun gave energy to the place, and we began again. New issues were posted, conversations commenced, but there was an edge. It seemed that on this day we would go into those dark and frightful places that had perhaps been visited before, but now we would go deeply. To set the tone, one of our number noted that there had been yet more killing in that land they called home. As the morning progressed, the clouds came, and by noon the Sun was completely hidden. A cool breeze brought a chill. Over the afternoon, it became darker and colder in stark contrast to the heat and intensity of the conversations. By late afternoon, I found myself sitting on a bank of steps in front of the villa, between two large groups in heated debate. I could hear some of the words, but didn't need to listen in order to catch the tones of anger, despair, fear, frustration, acid discontent and pain. It was deep and it went deeper.

---

28 The Talking Stick comes from the tradition of Native Americans. It involves passing a stick (sometimes highly decorated) around the circle of participants. Who ever holds the stick may talk, and those who do not hold the stick will listen, in both cases, with respect.

Shortly after 5 p.m. I rang some bells signaling Evening News. Nobody was listening, and the waves of pain and fear rolled on. There was nothing to do but simply be there with it all. After all, this was why we came together.

Sometime later, I do not know when, the conversation ceased, only to be replaced with an awesome silence. For practical reasons, it was not possible to return to the pavilion for Evening News; instead we gathered in a garden, sitting formally in white lawn chairs. The circle was no bigger, or smaller, than previously—but the distance between us all was huge. It appeared almost as the Theater of the Absurd, surreal and menacing. Dark clouds, chilled air, white chairs, green grass, somber people. I passed the talking stick—an olive branch—wondering whether it would simply wilt in the atmosphere. Most people just passed it along without saying a word. Many of those who spoke noted the difference between that moment and the evening before. Some voiced a feeling that all of us had. Yesterday had been but an illusion, a phantasm, a terrible ironic dream which would haunt us even as it disappeared. Evening News was over, and the group scattered, some walking alone, others with a friend or two. It was very quiet.

That night, after a meal I hardly touched, I went to my room, which was located just to one side of our pavilion where once again we would meet in the morning. The pavilion was lighted all through the night, illuminating a silent circle of 50 chairs. And over the top of the pavilion, I could see the dome of St. Peter's bathed in floodlights standing silently as it had for centuries. If I slept that night, I can't remember. I do not know what the others felt as they wrestled with the night, but I knew waves of fear and anger, fear and desperation. What had started as a glimmer of hope just two days before now seemed but a haunting, ironic nightmare.

And yet through it all I knew that the hope had been real, the space had been open, we had seen some light. But all of that had been followed by a forbidding darkness which threatened, or perhaps had succeeded, in quenching the light. It became clear that the end to our story was a matter of our choosing. We could see only light quenched by darkness and choose to live in that darkness. Or we could see that it was only because we had known the light and hope that we had been able to go deeply into the darkness. And so we could carry both the light and the darkness and continue the journey with a friend—remembering to sing. Our choice. Some words from Rumi, the Sufi poet, came to my mind. "There is a field, beyond right doing and wrong doing. I will meet you there."

The night ended and the dawn broke, and once again we were sitting in a circle, 50 Palestinians and Israelis, on our final day together. I opened the circle with a few words. Exactly what they were, I can't remember, but something like, We have known some hope and light together. We have entered into the darkness. This is a day of choosing. I propose that we take the next hour to be with our selves and/or talk with our friends. In one hour, I will ring the bells. Those who wish to return to our circle, please do so. Those who find that they cannot come back, for whatever reason, know that their choice is honored and respected. Then I said the words of Rumi one more time. "There is a field beyond right doing and wrong doing. I will meet you there." And I left.

Over the hour, I walked the grounds, past the olive trees, down the many paths, pausing to gaze at the looming Basilica of St. Peters. Strangely silent. Strangely comforting. Others were around, but I spoke to no one, and no one spoke to me. As the hour ended, I passed an olive tree. It gave me a fresh branch. I started ringing the bell and slowly returned to the circle of 50 chairs, not having a clue as to what might happen next.

I was surprised to see all the chairs full. My words were few, "We have known the light and walked in the darkness. And where are you my friends? Where are you going, and what are you going to do?" I passed the fresh olive branch to my right.

For the next several hours, people spoke, one at a time, with respect. As the hours passed, people came and went as they needed, but they always returned. There were tears and laughter. New projects were announced, and old ones revisited. Commitments were made to continue, and the roughness of the journey ahead acknowledged.

On this last day we had been joined by a special guest, the head of the Islamic community in Rome. And after all had spoken, I invited him to speak. He was introduced by David Rosen, a leading Orthodox Rabbi from Jerusalem. As I remember his words were something like, "The Koran teaches us that to kill one person is to kill us all. And to save one person is to save the world. We must take whatever steps we can." When he finished, there was absolute silence, and I asked the group to stand, and one more time look into the eyes of each of their fellows. It was a long look. And then I asked that they turn in place so that each person faced outwards to all points of the compass. I wished them well on their journey, and asked that they remember when they felt lonely and discouraged, that there was much love and respect behind them, at least at this moment. The circle broke. We had lunch.

The afternoon was an incredible flow of informal discussions, moments of reflection, relaxation. Dinner came, musicians from Palestine and Israel performed, people danced. And in the morning busses and taxis departed. I returned from Rome last night, and this morning I read that more have been killed. The struggle goes on, but I do not think it is hopeless. At the very least we all have a choice.

A Participant's Reaction

My comments come with all the biases of years of Open Space experience, to say nothing of a certain proprietary interest as the originator. One of the participants, Peera Chodorov, a first timer in Open Space, and also a Senior Advisor to an Israeli Cabinet Minister, made the following comments (quoted with permission):

> "Today, I am persuaded that the Open Space technique used at the conference was pivotal to its success. I am still processing the deep and rapid developments that took place within three days, evidence of which can be found in the continuing contact between the participants and the spirit of mutual commitment that was created. The positive experience highlighted the importance of delegating responsibility to the participants and their ability to conduct the meeting, rather than be controlled by pre-designated plans.
>
> The human and intellectual openness of the Open Space promoted attentiveness and helped the two sides abandon the positions in which they were respectively entrenched, in an effort to connect one with the other and develop an awareness of the individual hardships perpetrated by the conflict. The

same responsibility that each of the participants was given shaped the ties established and that still continue, by means of e-mails and, not less, through telephone calls. Also, we met in Tel Aviv, and we plan the continuation of what started in Rome.

I am toying with an imaginary idea, of an Open Space encounter between Sharon and Arafat, without pre-organized schedules and agendas, outlining what subjects can or cannot be discussed. In my mind, I can see how they are both smiling and hugging one another, if nothing else but for a photo-opportunity together. After all, how different are they from us? Mostly because they totally lost their own space and are controlled by their assistants, advisors and body-guards who also have lost their own space. How sad.

Harrison, I must confess that at the morning meeting of the first day, in the open circle at the villa in Rome, I was somewhat skeptical of the system, and when we got up for the first assignment, to choose the debating group to which we would be assigned, I felt it would not work. Very quickly I fell in love, and am still in love, with the idea.

The visual memory etched in my mind: smiling people, embracing, even kissing, a certain sense of intimacy in the "Open Space." I pray that we shall be able to safeguard this initial start, and succeed in imparting it to more and more people."

What happened in Rome is but an example. It did not bring Peace to the Middle East, and lasted but three days. For all those limitations, I believe the gathering is a significant example of Open Space at work, and more profoundly, the power and possibility of self-organization in the search for Peace. The "up front" organizing time was virtually zero, and all done under the most difficult conditions. And none of that pre-conference work had anything to do with what is typically the most labor intensive part, creating the agenda. Before the opening circle there was no agenda—hopes, fears, chaos, confusion and conflict in abundance—but no agenda.

The participants themselves spent no time engaged in activities designed to help them communicate, deal with conflict, reach consensus, build community, or any of the multitudinous "warm-ups" common to such gatherings. They came, just as they were, straight from the chaos of their lives in the Middle East, sat down, and within an hour and one half were hard at work on the major issues that confronted them.

It is not stretching a point to say that the participants did it all by themselves, at least in terms of the initiation and management of their discussions. At no point during our time together did I intervene in any way with any group. The issues were divisive, the conflicts real, of long duration, and the passions were high. But there was never a moment when the assembled body failed to handle this emotional time bomb.

Unlike a number of such gatherings, where participants are invited based on the likelihood that they would "get along," this group was invited because of its diversity, highly conflicted diversity. Certainly there were elements of both Palestinian and Israeli society that were not represented, but given the 50 "places at the table" (in the circle) it would be hard to imagine a more diverse group. From some points of view, it might even seem that the gathering was designed for failure. Bringing such a diverse, conflicted group together with no advance training, no agenda, no overt facilitation might almost seem irresponsible. Yet that is exactly what happened, and failure did not result.

Of all the things that happened in Rome, the most significant from my point of view, was the emergence of what I have called Genuine Community, which appeared not through the elimination of the chaos, confusion and conflict so obviously present, but rather through their inclusion and transcendence. To the best of my knowledge, every issue of import was laid on the table, and all were discussed with great heat and intensity, but by the end, a most remarkable thing had occurred, neatly caught in the phrase of Peera Chodorov quoted above. *"In conclusion, the visual memory etched in my mind: smiling people, embracing, even kissing, a certain sense of intimacy in the "Open Space".* We may not have achieved lasting Peace in the Middle East, but I think it fair to say that every person present experienced Peace that was in fact *the dynamic interrelationship of complex forces productive of wholeness, health and harmony.* And it happened, essentially, all by itself.

If this happened once, it could happen again, and the continuing experience with Open Space tells us that the events of Rome, while unique in their own way, are by no means an anomalous occurrence. There are no guarantees in this world, and not every story has a happy ending, but when it comes to enabling the conditions for Peace, I believe the tools are readily at hand, and need only be applied. That application is The Practice of Peace.

CHAPTER VI
The Practice of Peace

My version of the Practice of Peace starts with several caveats: First, never work harder than you have to; Second, Don't fix it if it ain't broke; And last (and most important), never delude yourself into thinking you are in control, even if the folks you are working with clamor for it. The exercise of arbitrary control in the name of Peace will produce the opposite.

PEACE BEGINS WITH YOU

Peace begins with you. I believe it was Gandhi who said you must be the change you wish to see in the world. Nowhere is this more true than in the critical task of Peacemaking. Words like authenticity and integrity point to essential qualities for all of life, but when the chosen endeavor is enabling Peace, those qualities gain importance rapidly. To the extent that what we say doesn't match what we do—we don't walk the talk—the Peace that we seek will disappear. The caveats I offer simply suggest certain things we might want to check before beginning the endeavor.

Never Work Harder than You Have to

This may sound like a prescription for laziness, given the workaholic, frenetic patterns that many of us adopt as we seek some sense of Peace in our lives, and our organizations. In a strange way, we do precisely the opposite of what we are seeking. It is perhaps no wonder that we fail to find what we are looking for. Working less, and being more, is the starting place for any practice of Peace.

At the simplest level, this is pure conservation of energy. The demands placed upon us when we take on the task of Peace are extreme. It is not just the many things that need doing, and the shortness of time available, it is also the ambient stress, strain and emotional overload that usually occur. A day in the service of Peace is rarely a walk in the park. Just as a marathon runner will never make the distance if the first mile is run in four minutes, so also with the Peacemaker. A good sense of pacing is critical.

There is also a deeper message here, I hope. Earlier I proposed that Peace is a process, not a thing; a journey and not a destination, that it is flow and not a state. Thus, while there are many bits and pieces critical to a peaceful life (adequate shelter, sufficient food, decent education, good roads, etc) none of them individually, nor all of them together, will get us where we want to go, unless they all fit and work together. Unless they flow, as it were. Most of us have had the experience of being "deprived" of what some might consider essentials for life, and yet still enjoyed remarkable Peace. I think of those times when I found myself in some remote environment, be that the American wilderness, or an African bush village. Not a toilet in sight, and light provided by the sun in the day and the moon by night. But I knew Peace in abundance.

Please understand, I find flush toilets useful, and electricity a positive advantage, but neither guarantees the presence of Peace, nor do their absence. The more I wish for the accouterments of civilization the less peaceful I become, and should I set about the hard work of laying pipe and stringing wire, I can almost guarantee that the natural flow of my environment will be interrupted. By remembering never to work harder than we have to, we create some space in which to enjoy Peace as it comes, and not as we might design it.

Don't Fix it If it Ain't Broke
All of which leads to the second caveat: *Don't fix it if it ain't broke.* I suppose this caveat could have broader application to our lives in general, but I am thinking specifically of our lives

as Peacemakers. If it is true that the process of self-organization works naturally towards the achievement of Peace (wholeness, health and harmony) and further, that this process has some 14 billion years' experience in the business, it might behoove us to pause a moment before attempting to fix it. As they say in the great State of Maine, "Don't fix it if it ain't broke." It could be (indeed I would take it as highly probable) that the perceived problem is one of our own making, very often related to some previous fix which was applied without fully understanding the nature of the system, and therefore the full implications of our fix.

Never Delude Yourself into Thinking You Are in Control

The last caveat is without doubt the most critical, difficult, and under some circumstances, painful. There is something in all of us that desperately wants to be in charge, particularly when things become chaotic, confusing and conflicted. When life seemingly runs out of control we feel the irresistible compulsion to set it right, restore order, and become once again the captain of our souls and master of our destiny. It is a lovely idea, but fatally flawed. For life at those times is not out of control, it is just being life. And life was not created for our personal pleasure and comfort. Storms come, rivers flood, volcanoes pop, businesses go kaput, and people die. All very much part of the natural order of things, no matter how much we might wish it were different. Adding insult to injury, the whole affair is so complex, fast moving and powerful that we would be lucky even to comprehend what is transpiring, let alone set everything right in a fashion that suits our sense of order. It won't happen, so don't even think about going there.

For the Peacemaker, this is a special challenge. By definition, we place ourselves in situations that are filled with pain and suffering, mental if not physical, but often both. Common human kindness would seem to dictate that we make every effort to mitigate the unpleasantness, relieve the suffering, banish the pain, especially if we can see the source clearly, and have the fix in mind. But that is not our job. To us it is given to stand as a Silent Witness, holding it all in our consciousness, including the suffering and the pain. There is no fix that we can devise that will set the situation right, no detailed program that will bring the people to the point they need to be, no new technology that will provide the magic button. And even if, by some lucky happenstance, such a panacea did come to our minds, it is not for us to do. Ours is a very different task, relating not so much to *doing* as *being*. Our function is to hold the space open so that the organization, or people with whom we work, can do what only it (or they) can do: be fully themselves, as a living, self-organizing system. Ultimately, they, and they alone, will heal themselves and find that wholeness, health and harmony that is Peace. Or not...And this is the truly hard part, for it may be that the end has come.

All living creatures have a life, which means that they also have a death. There is an end to all things. And when that end comes, sad as it may be, it is over. This is true for pussy cats, communities, corporations and countries. When it is over, it is over. We might wish that it weren't so, and resist in every possible way, but in the end, there is always an end. And as a Peacemaker, we are called upon to witness that ending as well. At such moments, it becomes crystal clear, if it had not been clear previously, that we are not in charge.

The role of the Peacemaker is unique, and all of us play it some of the time, and some of us play it most of the time. It is a special calling, but obviously not the only one. The process of life in all of its manifestations requires lots of *doing* as well. Plans must be made, projects initiated, programs managed, meals cooked, diapers changed, roofs constructed to protect us from the elements. Each of these activities is contributory, and all of them constitute the fabric of our lives. But none, individually or collectively, encompass the whole of life. There is more, and it is the special task of the Peacemaker to witness that whole in all of its aspects, beginning, middle and end.

THE HEART OF THE PRACTICE

The fundamental principle of the Practice of Peace is very simple: *Open space. Open space wherever, however, and as often as you can.* This is not only about the use of Open Space Technology, although that may be a good place to start. Rather, it is the conscious application of the power underlying Open Space Technology, self-organization.

Basic to this practice is the understanding that the organism is it own best healer, and the power behind that healing is self-organization. *Organism,* as I am using the word here applies to all living creatures and entities. That would include you and me as individuals, or all of us together in our collective manifestations known as *organizations* (families, communities, companies and countries). And when things fall apart, get out of whack, go over the edge, dissolve in chaos, all of which we experience as fragmentation, disease and discord (the very antithesis of Peace), putting Humpty Dumpty together again is not something that either we, or all the King's men, can accomplish. The task is too complex, made even more so by the rapidly changing environment in which everything takes place. But what is impossible for us is all in a day's work for the complex adaptive systems which we are, individually and collectively. The Practice of Peace, therefore, involves initiating, sustaining, and in some cases re-starting, that fundamental engine of our existence, self-organization.

OUR BODIES AS A MODEL AND A METAPHOR

For all of our infatuation with the so called miracles of modern medicine, the truth of the matter is that the greatest miracle is our body, and its capacity to sustain and regenerate itself. Our genetic code may provide the plan and the environment the necessary nutrient resources, but putting it all together and keeping it functional at some useful level is the gift of self-organization—at least that is the message I receive from the likes of Stuart Kauffman and his colleagues. And when it comes to the conquest of disease, it is obvious that Medicine has played an important role, but we sometimes seem to forget that this role is a *supportive* one. The super-star actor is, and always has been, our good old bodies.

Thirty years ago, I was privileged to work at the National Institutes of Health (NIH), the US Government agency responsible, directly and indirectly, for many of the advances in medicine. The work being done at the several Institutes, or at the many university centers the NIH supported, was truly exciting and often of a breakthrough nature. At the time it seemed possible to contemplate a cure for cancer and the elimination of heart disease and stroke. There was a certain euphoria in the air which clouded the basic recognition that, for all the improvements in the diagnosis and treatment of disease, it remained true that something like 95 % of all human ailments were self-limiting. Which is to say, 95 % of all of our afflictions will either get better by themselves or the experiment will terminate. The miracle of modern medicine would have no impact. Doubtless things have improved somewhat in 30 years, but for all the advances in Medicine it seems that the pathogens in our world have kept pace. HIV and AIDS for example, to say nothing of new strains of nasty critters who have found ways to resist and avoid our drugs. So on the basis of no firm evidence, I would be willing to bet that the old figure of 95 % still holds, more or less.

In the remaining 5 %, where medical knowledge and practice is effective, it is useful to consider what the effect actually is. We usually talk about "cure," but I think that may be stretching a bit. In fact, what medicine does is to give the body a boost so that it can do for itself (and can only do for itself) what it does quite naturally, heal itself. I suppose there are some exceptions when we get into the area of artificial organs, but, those situations are typically a means of buying time until the body can take over and do what it is meant to do.

There also seems to be a certain Jeffersonian quality to the practice of really good medicine. Thomas Jefferson proposed that "He who governs least governs best." In terms of our discussion, that might be rephrased as follows, "He or she who medicates least, medicates best." The point is to do as little as possible in order to achieve the desired effect, because any intervention can, and often does, have unintended, unforeseen and unfortunate consequences. A physician friend of mine once remarked that the science of medicine provided the knowledge, skills and techniques of "what" to do. The *art* of medicine lay in using all of the above appropriately to the situation, which always meant doing as little as possible.

At the end of the day, the body is what it has always been, a marvelous complex adaptive system, which under the majority of circumstances, self-organizes its way into an effective relationship with the external environment and itself, experienced as wholeness, health and harmony, otherwise known as Peace. This is not a static phenomenon, and at any given time there is an abundance of chaos, confusion and conflict, but in a most remarkable way, we all muddle through. And should we seek Peace of a different sort, characterized by stasis or equilibrium, it is certainly possible to eliminate that unholy trinity. But the final results may not be quite what we had in mind. Psychiatrist Arnold Mandell[29] notes that, "When you reach equilibrium in biology, you are dead."

Living with our bodies is an ongoing experience of self-organization. In the vast majority of circumstances, we don't have to plan a thing, and the organization of that incredible marvel of complex interactions is something to which we give nary a thought. It seems to happen pretty much all by itself. Order for free, as Kaufmann likes to remind us. Certainly there are unpleasant surprises along the way, some worse than others, which require more direct intervention, but if we are wise, that intervention will be as minimal as possible, lest the unintended consequences get the better of us. And when we fail to heed the inner wisdom of our bodies, seeking to supplant it with our own sense of how things ought to be done, we run the great risk of confusing everything, drowning in a cocktail of fixes, and fixes for the fixes, which all too often end up as dependence, addiction, or worse.

To say that the body's wisdom dictates doing as little as possible is not to suggest that we do nothing at all, for in fact there are a number of requirements when it comes to the care and feeding of our bodies. It is little more than adequate diet,

---

[29] Quoted in Gleick *op cit* pg 298.

sleep, exercise and avoid known hazards. And when we run into trouble, do as little as possible, basically just give the body some breathing space (Open Space) in which it can do what it does very well: heal itself.

Eventually bodies, as indeed everything else in the natural order, run out of steam. When it is over, it is over. We may wish it to be otherwise, but all good things come to an end. This ending may come as a surprise, but it shouldn't, for ending alone, amongst all the experiences and circumstances of our lives, is the only certain thing. Unprepared, this ending comes as rather a shock, but it needn't be. From the day we are born there is no question that we will die, and there are definite things we can do in order to ready ourselves. The care and feeding of our self-organizing system requires that we deal with the whole system in the moment, and over time, beginning, middle, end.

HEALING OUR COLLECTIVE (CORPORATE) BODIES

Analogies of all sorts are dangerous, but can be useful. The connection between our bodies and the body politic works for me in two respects. First, both are self-organizing systems. Secondly, each is its own best healer. I take the former as a matter of accepted fact, and the latter as a testable hypothesis, which if true makes the role of the Peacemaker possible And more importantly, allows us to utilize the enormous capacity of a self-organizing system to include and transcend chaos, confusion and conflict, thereby producing organizations characterized by wholeness, health and harmony, Peace. So please consider what follows as either the description of a future experiment or better yet, an experiment in progress. Personally, I believe we are well on the way, but with much still to be learned.

Simply put, when things fall apart, open space and allow healing to begin. The power resides not in opening space (or even less in Open Space Technology) but in the curative abilities of a self-organizing system. More accurately, therefore, the strategy is enabling the self-organizing system to do what it does quite naturally, all by itself. And that is where Open Space Technology comes in.

Open Space Technology is simply one way we have found to accomplish the task. It is not the only way, and doubtless we will discover better ways, but for a start it is a good one. It is effective in itself, and also leads to deeper learning about the ongoing Practice of Peace. Indeed I suspect that the major contribution of Open Space Technology may be in the latter arena, learning about the Practice of Peace. Peacemaking is an ongoing, every day affair, and if it could only be accomplished through the formal convening of an Open Space event, we would be in a very sorry state indeed. So I would suggest that where Open Space Technology is appropriate, use it. Where it is not appropriate (and that will be in the vast majority of situations we face), the experience of Open Space, i.e., opening a space, can be a very helpful guide to the enhancement of our Peacemaking efforts.

Open Space (Technology)—A Starting Point
I have briefly described the process, and detailed descriptions are available in my other books, so it is not my intent to cover all that ground one more time. Still less is it my intention to sell Open Space Technology. OST is free, and has been so from the beginning. I simply wish to offer, and to emphasize, my personal experience and the experience of many others.

When Peace is at risk, or has seemingly departed, the stakes become excruciatingly high. Time is short, need is great, resources are few and action is essential. Delay, even a small one, almost certainly guarantees that a bad situation will become worse. Under such circumstances, elaborate plans and complex procedures will fail, not because they are bad, or ill conceived. It is simply a question of time, or more to the point, the lack of it. In addition, when chaos, confusion and conflict turn into their negative counterparts of fragmentation, dis-ease and discord, our capacity to design and implement such things rapidly goes down hill. We need an effective first step, a starting place—fast!

When the choice is Open Space Technology, it all begins with *an invitation* to the people who care about the issues at hand. Doubtless they care about them in many different ways, which is at once the source of discord, and also the incredible resource for solution, which genuine diversity provides. In a wonderful way, the cause of the pain is also the nutrient material for solution. This is *everybody* who cares, what I call, *The Coalition of Concern.*

My use of the word invitation is not accidental. As much as we might like to grab the combatants by the scruff of the neck and bang some sense into their heads, that particular approach will have only a short lived effect on the level of hostilities. Violence replaced by violence only produces more of the same. Invitation, on the other hand, is open to refusal, which is at once risky (nobody will come) and energizing. Those who do come really want to be there.

Once present, invite everybody to sit in a circle. It may have to be a very big circle, even concentric circles, but a circle nonetheless. A circle is important. There is no hiding in a circle. Everybody faces everybody, face on. And a circle has neither a beginning nor an end, which means that there is no first place in a circle. All places are equal. A circle also defines a particular area, a space. It therefore provides focus and presence, and with both, there is a degree of safety. While nobody knows exactly what will happen next, they do know where the starting point resides: here and now.

It turns out that a circle of chairs is a marvelous mixer. People take their places in a random fashion depending on when they arrive and what chair is available. There is no special place for one group or another, and even though one or two friends/associates may arrive together, they will automatically sit next to others who are likely to be strangers, or from a different group. Without any overt effort, prior associations, social structures and organization are dis-aggregated.

Lastly, a circle of people, particularly a large circle, is awesome in the root sense of that word, awe inspiring. It also may be awful, in the sense that it is disconcerting and threatening. This may not be apparent to the casual onlooker who sees "just a circle of people," but those who sit in that circle have a different experience, particularly when the issue that brought them to that place is deeply troubling, and their fellows in that circle are strangers, or even historical enemies. It is one thing to sit in the family circle with all members known and familiar. It is quite a different thing when your colleagues are unknown, and/or presumed to be hostile.

The source of awe in the circle is not just the people who define its boundaries, it is what lies in between—nothing. The open space which commences at everybody's feet is strange for most, and terrifying for some. To understand this you have to be part of the circle, or just watch the behavior of the assembling group as the participants find their places, and you will see the obvious signs of aversive behavior. People will walk all the way around the circle rather than taking the shortest route across. Or if there is no other option than to cross the circle, they will scuttle hurriedly across, or make the passage in pairs. Those who find themselves standing at the edge of the circle will evidence a clear recognition as to where that edge is. Like small children on the edge of a cold swimming pool, they will stick in a toe and hastily retreat. What's going on here? What inspires this odd behavior? I think the answer is chaos.

In the center of the circle there is nothing. No order, no structure, no meaning, in short, no helpful signs telling us what to do. There is just nothing, or pure chaos, at least pure as it gets. Take away order, structure, and meaning, leaving only emptiness, or at best random and infinite possibilities representing all the things that could happen in that space, and you have chaos. And the people, literally and figuratively, are sitting at its edge.

Being at the edge of chaos is significant, not only as an emotional event, but more importantly as a, or perhaps *the,* critical precondition for the initiation of self-organization. You will remember Stuart Kaufmann's preconditions described above. Presuming he is correct in his observations, the group entering into Open Space finds itself with all conditions met, and all they have done is accept an invitation to sit in a circle.

They find themselves in a *relatively safe nutrient environment.* Even though the issues they face may be immense and seemingly intractable, fraught with dangers of every imaginable sort (remember the 50 Palestinians and Israelis), for the moment there is a safe resting place. Because the group assembled is a hodgepodge of interested parties, drawn together by their concern for the common issue, not the unity of their approach and feelings, it is guaranteed that there will be *high levels of diversity of elements and the potential for complex inter-relationships.* And their concern for that issue is not a matter of idle, academic interest. They are looking for solutions, resolution, improvement—something that will make sense out of their situation, restore wholeness, health and harmony amongst themselves and with their environment. In short, there is a genuine *search for fitness.* And last, but not least, the simple mechanics of sitting down in a circle has broken up any prior social connections (*sparse prior connections*). They are ready, and hardly a word has been spoken in any official sort of way.

That word does come in the form of the brief remarks of the facilitator. Like the catalyst in a chemical reaction, the word is small, hardly noticeable relative to the energy and activity it releases. Typically in something like fifteen minutes, the group is hard at work, creating its own organization, although giving little thought to the process of organizing. It seems to happen all by itself, and within an hour and a half the emergent organization is doing its job, no help needed. This is FAST! And it is effective, as our experience in Rome, and thousands of other places, demonstrates. None of this is to underestimate the level of effort required to find the place and get the people there. The organizers of the conference in Rome faced incredible obstacles and impossible time tables. But they did it, and it can be done. It is also noteworthy to remember what these brave souls did *not* have to do. There was no need for agenda building, facilitator training and acquisition, process development, or meeting management. Just get there and go!

The first step of a practice for Peace is to open space. With that accomplished, the power of self-organization takes over, and for the moment at least, little more is required. The predictable results, broadly speaking, are twofold. First, there is obvious accomplishment. Issues are addressed, and solutions found. Perhaps not completely or perfectly, but ordinarily, real progress is made. The fact of accomplishment in what many might have perceived as a hopeless situation has value vastly greater than the particulars. Which leads to the second, more important result—the return of hope, and with it respect and trust, all adding up to a genuine experience of Peace at work.

In highly conflicted situations the experience of Peace is such a rare commodity that people tend to forget what it was like. In places like The Middle East and Afghanistan where the struggles have lasted for decades, children grow up never knowing anything different, and understandably presume that the way things are is the only way they could be. Always more of the same. Whole belief systems, social structures, and daily life patterns emerge to deal with the situation, and in a bizarre fashion serve only to support its continuance. Since all these things operate largely at an unconscious level, the people involved understandably presume there is no other way. Presenting rational arguments for useful alternatives is always worth trying, but I think experience has shown that such an approach is largely ineffective. Nothing will change until it changes, then there is a different experience. And that is precisely what happens when space is opened. In the place of fragmentation, discord and dis-ease, one experiences wholeness, harmony and health. It can come as quite a shock.

It is worth noting that the continuing experience of the absence of Peace is not unique to the world of nations and peoples. Precisely the same thing happens at all levels of our social environment, and the results are identical. In the world of business and industry, war between labor and management becomes a way of life, and even in the supposedly altruistic environment of nonprofits and NGOs the situation is the same. All of which makes the point that the role of the Peacemaker is not simply an international one. No matter the social level, the experience of fragmentation, discord and dis-ease are well known, and little will change until the experience changes. Seemingly this produces an insoluble "chicken and egg" problem. Until we can glue the pieces together, eliminate the discord, and cure the dis-ease, we will never know Peace, but none of those things can occur until Peace exists. We have tried the "step at a time" approach, but we never quite seem to get ahead of the game—always a day late and a dollar short. When we open space (invoke self-organization), a small step becomes a huge leap. We find ourselves already present in what appeared to be an unattainable vision. A first step has been taken.

Reflection

When space is opened and self-organization begins, a group will find itself experiencing what many presumed to be unattainable. Furthermore, it all happens very quickly, and without apparent effort. An interesting, and certainly very natural reaction is not to notice what has occurred, or if noticed then presume that it is a trick, even a hallucination. It seems to be a law of perception that you only notice what you are prepared to see, and if all your prior experience tells you that what you are looking at simply can't happen, it is highly likely that the entire experience will pass you by. This phenomenon does not affect the quality of work done, the solutions devised, or the problems solved in the course of the open space. But if Peace is to become something more than a brief episode, it is helpful to notice it (anchor the experience) as it passes by.

Assisting a group of people to notice their experience need not be a major effort, and it probably should not be initiated while the group is actually working. At that point it is sufficient that they have the experience, even if unconscious of it. In fact, interrupting the work with suggestions that they notice what is going on is quite likely to impair both the quality of the work and the experience itself. However, at the conclusion, I find it very possible and useful to pause for reflection before the group disbands. A few well chosen questions usually suffice. What was strange, what was different about their experience? What surprised? What energized? Did they notice that they went from a standing start to full operation in a very brief time? Did anybody have fun?

Fun, it turns out, is an unmistakable mark of productive work, even when the task is terribly serious, and maybe even painful. Somewhere along the line, our world made a radical distinction between work and play (fun) to the point that work is never play, and having fun is a clear indication that you are not working. I find this to be a profound error. At a personal level I have never done anything useful that was not, in some significant way, fun. More generally, I always listen for laughter in the course of any Open Space I facilitate. When it occurs, and it always seems to, I know that everything is working just fine. We assume such behavior just can't happen. But when it does, something is really different, and that is well worth noticing.

The point of reflection (and it may only take five minutes) is to lay the groundwork for what can happen next. What happened once could happen again, made even more likely if it is not inhibited by our blinders of disbelief. In a word, the experience of Peace must be moved from the category of The Impossible to that of The Expected. This is not to be confused with wishful thinking, or some new version of the old power of positive thought. It is a simple fact that when we think something to be impossible, or worse don't know that it could exist, we don't even try. If Peace is to become a continuing reality, it must be tried over and over again. And the more we try the better we become at the task of Peacemaking, and living in Peace. In the practice of Peace, as elsewhere, practice is important.

Practicing Peace

The third step in the practice is to practice what we learn, and learn what we practice. Which is a rather convoluted way of saying that we need to make Peace and Peacemaking a conscious act. Peacemaking needs to become an everyday, ongoing occurrence, and not only that special effort mounted when disaster destroys our carefully constructed world. It remains true that the major engines of Peace and Peacemaking are not of our creation or doing. Self-organization will continue to happen all by itself and Grief will do its work. But there is any number of things that we can do, or more often *not do,* which substantially raise the odds of the appearance of Peace.

Many people who have used Open Space Technology over the years (me included) discovered that in addition to being a powerful and effective tool for enhanced collaborative effort, it was also a very fundamental and useful approach to everyday life in all of its manifestations, large and small. This has given rise to what some of us have called, "The Open

Space Mentality." We tend to use these words cautiously, if only because taken out of context they sound more like a mental aberration ("spaced out") than anything useful. But the point is a simple one. Using the insights and principles of Open Space every day enables us to have better and more peaceful days. This is a personal experience, we feel better and more peaceful. It is also a professional experience. Our work in the world seems to enable others to have better and more peaceful days. The critical elements, as I have experienced them, are:

1) Invitation

2) Circle

3) Passion and Responsibility

4) Remember the Four Principles

5) Observe the Law

6) Keep Grief Working

Invitation

When activities are begun with an invitation, the space is truly open for all sorts of possibilities. Invitation is permissive, which means, among other things, it can be refused. Of course, permissiveness in some circles is abhorrent based on the assumption that if everybody did just what they wanted to do, nothing useful would get done. Doubtless there is some truth behind this assumption, but it also exacts a considerable price. When we assume the worst, we often get it. Or put slightly differently, people very often will live *down* to our lowest expectations. You might also ask yourself if you have ever seen anybody do a truly good job that they did not want to do. Invitation provides the space for those who truly care to step forward, and those who step forward have made a commitment to care. There is a definite risk with an invitation, but also many rewards. Primary among these is the dignity and respect conferred upon those who are invited. Extending an invitation acknowledges what would be true in any case, that those invited are free, consenting individuals. At the opening of any enterprise, who would want anything less?

Circle

The power of the circle has been known for millennia, and certainly is not the exclusive preserve of Open Space Technology. Shamans the world over, King Arthur (of Knights of Round Table fame) and most families (as in family circle), understand that when important things are to be accomplished, they are best done in a circle of peers, comrades and colleagues. When we line people up in rows, as in a classroom, we set the stage for passive/aggressive behavior. There is seemingly no choice but to sit still, shut up and take notes. And the power position is clear. The person standing in front, facing the (one hopes) docile crowd is obviously the expert. All others are clearly less well equipped. This is not the geometry of creativity, and other shapes, such as squares and rectangles, are not noticeably better. Placing people at a table instantly creates the conditions for negotiation. Inevitably we speak of "our side," and "your side." And we look to the head of the table to discover who is in charge. This is the geometry of conflict and opposition, and if neither exist at the start, it is likely that both will emerge. The circle avoids all of the above automatically, without fuss, bother or any words of instruction. And best of all is a circle with nothing in the middle. No tables, instructional devices, extra chairs. nothing in the way, and everybody present, eyeball to eyeball.

Several years ago, people at the Bank of Montreal (Canada), having experienced a number of Open Space events, decided that tables were out, at least tables in their meeting rooms. Just a circle of chairs which could be expanded or contracted as need dictated. One day, however, somebody made a scheduling mistake, and the management in a particular branch found it necessary to borrow some space from a neighboring company, which came complete with a large conference table anchored securely in the middle of the room. Not thinking anything about it, the managers gathered for their meeting, taking their places at the table. At the conclusion of the two hour session, the participants departed, all in foul temper. What was to have been a simple, straight forward meeting had turned into a nasty disaster. And everybody knew who the culprit was, the table.

Silly story with a major point, I think. For me the fundamental geometry for Peacemaking is a circle, with nothing in the way. And certainly not a table. At the very least one avoids the agony of the Peace negotiations between North and South Korea where it seemed necessary to argue about the shape of the table for several years. I suppose argument is better than shooting each other, but I am not sure that it advanced the cause of Peace. Peace begins when people are ready to make Peace, and a good indication that all parties are in that state of readiness is their willingness to sit in a circle.

Passion and Responsibility

One of the rituals of every Open Space event is that the participants are invited to identify all of the issues and opportunities pertinent to their gathering for which they personally have some genuine passion and are willing to take responsibility. Responsibility might mean leading a session on that subject, and following up (if need be) on implementation of solutions that pertain to it. This makes the point that Open Space is not just another form of Brainstorming, where typically people think of good ideas which somebody else can carry out.

How we came to the idea of passion and responsibility, I can't remember. I suppose it just seemed like a good idea at the time. But over the years it has proved to be infinitely more than a "good idea." Profound insight, (for which nobody, certainly not me, can take credit) would be much closer to the mark.

It often seems in various Peacemaking efforts that major attention is devoted to the elimination, or at least calming of passion, as if it were passion that got us into trouble. There is no question that when passions subside, the situation appears more pacific, but I think that is an illusion. More often, the passion has simply gone underground, only to appear in more destructive forms. Or if the passion has truly departed, the situation is not so much pacific as dead. Nothing moves, nothing happens. It just sits. For better or worse, passion— our human care and concern—is what makes the world, at least our world, go around.

Unfettered passion, however, can be a problem. And so we invite passion bounded by responsibility. If you have the passion, take responsibility, and if you are not willing to do that, don't bring it up. This is not about moral "oughts and shoulds" but simple practicality. Passion without responsibility is just a flash in the pan, all light and sound, but no go. Of course, responsibility without passion is just drudgery and duty. It doesn't go anywhere either. But together, passion *with* responsibility, then we really have something.

With passion and responsibility, things can become truly exciting, sometimes too much so, particularly when there are conflicting passions, albeit responsible ones. Unattended, conflicting passions tend to produce deadlock or explosion, but neither is inevitable. The solution is simple, just open more space. We tend to think of space in purely physical terms, and when understood that way, space is definitely a limited commodity, which makes the business of opening more space appear impossible. After all there is only so much available. The Middle East is a perfect example where we find many diverse people, lots of passions, and a limited supply of real estate, all of which could be used to support a fatalist's position that Peace in the Middle East can never happen. The fatalist in our midst may well be correct, but not because of the limitations imposed by finite physical space.

Space comes in many varieties including emotional space (a place for my feelings) intellectual space (tolerance and respect for differing ideas), cyberspace, and I am sure many more. Speaking only for myself, I find that physical space, while important, is perhaps the least critical of all the varieties of space. New York City, for example has more people than Israel and Palestine, less land, and yet for a couple of hundred years has been remarkably peaceful. Outsiders, such as my self, may find New Yorkers to be a cantankerous bunch, but in a remarkable and sustainable way, it all works. I think the secret is that there is a tradition of giving each other the space they need.

Providing essential space to others is a critical part of the Peacemaking process, and I think it is a skill we may learn and practice. You might call it being spacious, and just as we all know people who are gracious, so also spacious. Indeed, I find that being spacious is an integral part of being gracious.

In the presence of truly gracious people, there always seems to be the room to be just the way you are, even if a little odd. Graciousness is an essential characteristic of any good host or hostess, which is why their parties always seem to be rich, full and interesting. I suggest that "gracious spaciousness" is equally important in that largest of all parties, life together here on Planet Earth. And for the Peacemaker it may be the most important thing we bring to that marvelous party.

Remember the Four Principles

At the beginning of every Open Space event, four principles are outlined as guidelines for the participants. These principles are not offered as prescriptions for behavior, but rather in recognition that the conditions cited are going to exist no matter what. Although many might consider them antithetical to "proper meeting management," the conditions are in fact contributory, and therefore should be accepted without feeling guilty that we have shirked our duty. The Four Principles are:

- Whoever comes is the right people.

- Whatever happens is the only thing that could have.

- Whenever it starts is the right time.

- When it is over it is over.

These principles constitute useful reminders to the participants and facilitator alike as they go about the task of Peacemaking. I think therefore that they may find an important place in a Practice of Peace, if only because they appear to me to be the working principles of any well functioning self-organizing system.

The first principle, *Whoever comes is the right people,* is a simple, albeit ungrammatical, recognition of the obvious fact that the people assembled are the only ones present. What makes these people the *right people* is the fact that they cared enough to come. These people are the Coalition of Concern, or at least the beginning of it, and the fact that they care is the only required ticket for admission. Of course, they may care in many different ways, which is at once a source of conflict and the resource for solution, for it is out of the rich diversity of thoughts and feelings that new solutions emerge.

Obviously there may also be multitudes of other folks who also care about the issue at hand (whatever it might be), but they did not care sufficiently to come. This does not make them bad people, inadequate, morally inferior, or deserving any other judgment. Doubtless, there are good reasons, and perhaps they will come the next time, and the Coalition of Concern will grow. But this time the fact remains, whoever comes is the right people because they cared enough to come. Worrying about all the absentees can only dilute the powerful possibilities already present.

For the Practice of Peace in the broader environment of our troubled world, much time, effort and anxiety could be saved were we to stop worrying about getting the "right people" (defined usually as those with the positional title and authority). Start with the ones who care and the rest will come, or not. But make a start. The initial effort may seem small and inconsequential, but our growing understanding of Living Systems teaches us that everything is connected, and all are integrally related. So start anywhere and eventually you *can* impact the whole. But there are still no guarantees. It may also be that the end is at hand, and even if the "right" (politically correct) people were in attendance, nothing could be done. But you do not know that. So start where you can start and you will more than likely discover that whoever comes is the right people, and, in any case, they are the only ones there.

The second principle, *Whatever happens is the only thing that could have,* could be taken as the mournful cry of a convinced fatalist, but once again it is only a simple recognition of the actual state of affairs which cuts through all of the "could-have-beens, might-have-beens, should-have beens, and if-onlies," bringing us into sharply into the present moment, right NOW. And Now is all we have. By definition, the past is over and the future hasn't happened yet. We can remember, and we can dream, but where we live is now. Those who live only in their dreams or their memories tend towards the ineffective, and they miss all of the incredible stuff, good and bad, happening Now. Not very complicated, but most important for the Peacemaker. Dreams of Peace and memories of Peace all have their place, but until or unless we have Peace now, it doesn't matter very much.

Now, it turns out, is expandable.[30] To understand this we might start by looking at the opposite, a "skinny" Now. And some people have very skinny Nows. They are perpetually worried about the future and regretful of the past, and their sense of Now grows smaller and smaller until there is hardly anything there at all. And the smaller it gets, the more frantic they become, trying to squeeze every last bit into an infinitesimally small Now.

---

[30] The notion of an expanding Now is by no means unique to me. However, I have written on the subject. See *Expanding Our Now: The Story of Open Space Technology,* Berrett-Koehler, 1997.

Other people treat life in a very different mode. They seem to have oceans of time and space through which they flow in a maddeningly relaxed fashion. I suppose there are multiple ways of talking about this, but to my eyes, these people have very big Nows. And they have the capacity to expand those Nows almost at will so that past and future link seamlessly with the present moment. In practical terms this means that dreams are not something that might happen someday, rather they are a present reality in the process of unfolding. And memories are not things that have moved beyond our reach, but rather constant companions available for our reflection and instruction. When Now becomes very big (or even gets just a little bigger) there is a calming sense of wholeness, integration and completeness, Peace. Getting from here (small Now) to there (big Now) is an interesting journey, which starts like all journeys with a single step, taken right now. And that all becomes possible when we recall the principle, *Whatever happens is the only thing that could have.*

The third principle, *Whenever it starts is the right time,* flies flagrantly in the face of all those who think they are in charge, want to be in charge, or are sure that somebody ought to be in charge. Such people presume that the essence of control is to determine the schedule, and of course, they assume the right time is *their* time. Like all of the other principles, this is not a prescription for desired behaviors, but rather a simple observation of fact. Nothing has ever started "on time." Even something as carefully managed (controlled) as a NASA launch starts when it starts. In the messier areas of our lives things get even worse (or better, from some points of view). The carefully scripted meeting with schedules broken down into five minute increments is typically off schedule from the moment it begins, and goes down hill from there. And when we come to the really juicy places of life, involving such things as inspiration and creativity, you can just forget about the clock. The important thing to notice here is that such things as clocks and schedules are external and arbitrary, having only a loose association with what actually goes on, and certainly don't control it. Even more critical is the fact that when we concentrate on clocks and schedules, we lose sight of the living reality of the organic systems which we are, and of which we are a part. Open, living, self-organizing systems are never "on time," they are their own time. For the Peacemaker this understanding is core. Peace, like all other fundamental realities of life, never happens on schedule, it happens when it happens. *Whenever it starts is the right time.*

The final principle, *When it is over it is over,* can be a very tough pill to swallow, particularly when you have invested your heart, soul, nights and weekends in search of Peace. But sometimes, things don't work out. Despite maximum best efforts, the patient died. It is possible, of course, to continue the agony, thinking of all of the "what ifs" and "if onlies," but the stark fact of the matter is, it didn't work. Somewhere in the great calculus of life and energy, we came up with a zero. Nada. Nothing. Zilch. Obviously there can be useful lessons to be learned in what may seem like a failure, and those lessons should be taken seriously, but once the post mortem is done, hanging on to what could have been is a lose/lose game. It is time to let go and move on. As the writer of Ecclesiastes reminds us, there is a time for everything—sowing, reaping, dying. Human beings find this awkward, and definitely not according to our plans, not on our agenda, so to speak. But it is useful to remember occasionally that the plans and the agenda ultimately are not our own. We are not in charge; we never have been in charge. And, as long as we remain attached to what has ended, we are not available for what is starting. Dealing with the strong feelings involved, and getting ready to move on is never easy, however Griefwork, as we've discussed, gives us powerful and effective means to deal with all that painful stuff.

Observe the Law

One of the stranger aspects of an Open Space event is *The Law of Two Feet,* which is explained with humor by the facilitator during a short introduction. Although the law is quite serious, it is a rather different sort of law, commanding us to do what most of us would prefer to do anyhow and in fact do, but usually secretively and with a sense of guilt. The law says, *"If at any time, during our time together you find yourself in any situation where you are neither learning nor contributing, use your two feet. Go somewhere else. Do something useful, and for sure don't waste time feeling miserable."*

Upon first hearing, participants often cannot believe their ears, for they are being instructed to do what years of parental admonitions and rules of school teachers and administrators have made quite clear is unacceptable. Here, we are encouraged to leave any situation which is unproductive for us, or where we are not contributing productively. Positively rude! However, despite the social strictures, using our two feet, metaphorically if not physically, is something we do all the time and secretly wish we could do more. When things get dull, boring and stupid we discover our hearts and minds totally somewhere else. Only our bodies remain, and if the situation goes on long enough, even the old body does its best to disappear, all the while remaining in place, a condition usually marked by loud snores. So the Law of Two Feet is not unknown, and in fact is usually observed, albeit covertly.

What would happen were we to make the covert explicit and acceptable? A lot of good things, as it turns out. First of all, we could immediately stop feeling guilty about what we were going to do anyhow. Guilt not only feels bad, but is also a terrible waste of energy. That energy could be better deployed elsewhere. There is something marvelously refreshing when you strike a blow for freedom and simply accept yourself as you actually are. It is called authenticity.

The Law of Two Feet, however, makes more important contributions than the simple elimination of our personal pain and discomfort. It is actually lifts the functionality of any group. The secret is the removal of negative energy, that blah feeling which occurs when some members of the group are sitting there head in hand, nodding off, or worse yet, cantankerously debating inane points to no purpose, simply because they are bored. Other members may be deeply interested and actively engaged, but the dark cloud of the blahs is very hard to ignore or overcome. If only those disaffected souls would leave! And when they do, it is amazing how spirits and productivity soar. Score one for The Law of Two Feet!

When the disaffected do depart, they are then freed to make their own contributions in areas more to their liking. The conventional wisdom insists, rather blindly I think, that if folks just walked off when they got bored, society would be in a sorry state. Certainly meeting managers, and other keepers of the corporate weal would be sorry (or perhaps secretly relieved), but for society, I believe the net gain can be enormous. It is true that there are different strokes for different folks, which is only a shorthand way of acknowledging that we are not all interested in the same thing, or competent in the same way, and thank God for that.

Fortunately, there are lots and lots of people, and it is usually the case that someone somewhere is the right person for the job, it remains only for job and person to be connected. Making that connection becomes infinitely easier when you have a number of people searching about for something useful to do which will fit both their interests and their talents. This is called the *Search for Fitness,* which as you will recall is not only a critical engine of Darwinian Evolution, but also one of Stuart Kaufmann's essential preconditions for self-organization.

In a word, the Law of Two Feet both acknowledges and facilitates one of the core processes of our life and (if we are correct) the central mechanism of Peacemaking, self-organization. When self-organization grinds to a halt, productivity and creativity cease. Most importantly, Peace, as I have been describing it, becomes questionable, if not impossible.

For the Peacemaker in all of us, applying the Law of Two Feet as we engage our task and work our strategy may appear problematic. Thoughts of duty, discipline and commitment seemingly dictate that we do just the opposite—stick it out, never run, endure, endure, endure. Our personal sense of comfort is not to be considered, and above everything else never leave just because you are bored. Obviously, there is something admirable about such thoughts and actions, but I also suspect that they are more than a little misguided, representing a misunderstanding of the nature of the task, and our potential contribution to it. In our central role as *Witness,* it is not our function or responsibility to create Peace, but rather to enable the conditions under which Peace may occur. In most cases, this means doing little and being much. As we all know, or will quickly discover, doing little and being much is exceptionally hard work. As long as we are able, we should certainly put our nose to the grindstone, metaphorically speaking. But when that ability wanes, and our energy dissipates (often first manifest as a feeling of boredom and disinterest), sticking around serves no good purpose. Best to use the two feet and search for something meaningful to do or be. This could be just taking a deep breath or a long walk in the woods, both of which may be our greatest service to Peace, and our best strategy for allowing it to appear.

One final observation from Open Space and, I think, an important learning for our Practice of Peace. I, and many others, have noticed over the years that although conflict may be intense and vigorous, never has the group been unable to handle that conflict, and more importantly, they have always learned deeply from the incident. In no case was it necessary for me as the facilitator to intervene in any overt fashion, because the group handled the situation all by itself. It should also be noted that no effort was made prior to the gathering to train the group in so-called conflict resolution skills. The results were the same whether or not the group had had extensive training in this area, or none at all. An obvious and persisting question has been, why is this so?

Some have suggested that the clue lay in my personal presence. I do not doubt that my presence contributed something to the life of the group, but it is also true that many other facilitators, with a very different personal presence, have experienced similar results. So the question, so far as I am concerned, remains to be answered. After some long time thinking about it, I have concluded that the hero is none other than The Law of Two Feet.

At a very practical level, I take it to be true that no person (other than the pathologically deranged) actually likes to lose their cool and engage in violent conflict. The problem arises when a person becomes locked in an unpleasant situation with no obvious alternatives. Were they to leave, cool off and gain perspective, they would probably do so. And since they presumably cared deeply about the issue at hand (hence the conflict), there is a high likelihood that they would return to the discussion once they were in a better frame of mind. The Law of Two Feet, of course, provides precisely the needed open door. And it swings both ways, in and out. Is this really the answer? Who knows, but it certainly accounts for the observed behavior.

Presuming there is some validity to my conclusion, I think there are some profound implications relating to the function of a self-organizing system. The process of self-organization seemingly stops, or badly falters, when external control is exercised, and room for movement is restricted or closed. As soon as the space is open, the process seems to continue, or restart. The Law of Two Feet, therefore not only makes for more productive (non-destructive) meetings, and enables people to feel better, but it does so by safeguarding the first essential pre-condition of self-organization (ala Kaufmann) *a relatively safe nutrient environment* or we might say space—a space sufficient to move around in.

I will boldly suggest that observing The Law of Two Feet in all Peacemaking situations (in addition to the narrower Open Space Event) will have a more than salutary effect on our efforts. I understand that this represents something of a departure from what sometimes appears as almost a normative approach in which the combatants are locked in a room with little food and a facilitator whose task it is to restore Peace, usually by telling everybody what to do. And further, when everybody agrees to play nicely, they may rejoin polite society. Overstatement for sure, but not totally off the mark, at least in a number of situations in my experience, and more in my knowledge. And the alternative? Well I think we have been describing the alternative. Open space and let the Law of Two Feet rule. Given the room and the freedom to move, the complex adaptive system will do what it is very good at: create wholeness, health and harmony. We call that Peace.

Keep Grief Working

Griefwork, as we have noted, can perform its function of removing the natural toxic byproducts of self-organization without assistance, even as the process of birth can work without physician or midwife. And probably in the majority of situations, Griefwork will do what it has done for millennia without help. That said, there are a number of things that can be done to ease the process and enhance the probabilities of a positive and speedy outcome as each stage of Griefwork passes. Being fully present through Shock and Anger, Denial, Memories, Despair, Silence and Vision is a special opportunity for the Peacemaker.

The Role of the Peacemaker — Shock and Anger

In the face of shock and anger the Peacemaker will do nothing, for nothing can be done, except to create and maintain the space in which the shock and anger may roll and do its essential work. This is the role of Witness. I have alluded to this role previously, but it is now time to spell it out in further detail.

The Witness appears to do little or nothing, for the central contribution is less about doing than being. Those who play this role (and all of us can, though some better than others) make themselves present in the moment with such intensity and power that no words or actions are required. We recognize such people not because of their sagacious wisdom expressed in pithy phrases, but simply because they are inescapably there. No matter what happens, or how stormy the moment, their unmistakable presence seems everywhere. Like a beacon in a rough sea, or a strong tree in a high wind, they give us our bearings and provide grounding, even as we are being swept off our feet. At one and the same time, they appear as intimate to us as our own breath, and yet somehow above it all, anchored in some transcendent place. Without blame or judgment, the Witness simply accepts the shock and anger as it is. No attempt at rationalization or pacification, just accepted as it is. Not an easy job for sure, but essential if the space is to be kept open so that the people can catch their breath.

Denial

In the presence of Denial, the special role of Witness is indispensable and in some ways even more difficult than in the prior situation with shock and anger. In the prior situation the natural flow of adrenaline, occasioned by the crisis and its aftermath, may be sufficient to sustain focus and presence. When Denial takes over, the enemy is tedium, more of the same old, same old, apparently going nowhere. But the process is working, and as the pain fades and the wound heals, it becomes possible to move on. But where to? Here the continuing presence of the Witness can be critical. Without saying a word, or doing a thing, the Witness provides that quiet grounding in reality that offers a starting point. This is not about suggesting a future, creating the plans, offering direct assistance, but it is all about marking the spot of commencement. Here. Now.

Memories

This is a point where the work of the Peacemaker may move clearly and usefully beyond the role of silent Witness. I find it very possible and effective to create special places which invite the telling of the tale. The Irish, of course, have reduced all this to a fine art in an ancient ritual known as The Wake. Upon the death of a person, family members, friends and usually others as well, gather at the local pub. And the tale is told, and told, and told. The good times and the bad, the funny events and the sad—all find their place. And when the tale is told, or the Guinness runs out, it is not unusual that the sun will also be rising. But the work has been done.

Despair

For the Peacemaker, being present at the moment of Despair is a peculiar challenge. On the one hand, our normal (at least I hope it is normal) concern and empathy for others draws us into their pain, until it almost becomes our pain. For them, and probably also for ourselves, we wish desperately for alternatives, some surcease to the obvious suffering. At such a time it is not uncommon to hear words like, "Don't despair," as if the despairing had any choice. But somehow it seems the right thing to do. Draw them away from their pain, and almost like small children, kiss it and make it all better. And yet it is precisely the pain that provides the motivation for deliverance. Rather than avoid it (which they can't) they have to go through it. It is the only way to the other side. And so our words, if any words are necessary, should be something like, "Please Despair with great vigor!"

Truthfully words at such a moment are hardly helpful, at least words of rational argument, or logical persuasion. There is logic to the process of grief and it certainly can be helpful to understand what is going on. But in the moment, logic and understanding are nowhere to be found, blotted out by a searing cloud of pain. But what logic will not reach, presence can, and once again the role of the Silent Witness comes to the fore. In truth there is nothing to be done, for the person, or group, must do it all for themselves. Only they can let go, but having a warm hand to hold in the process is good.

Silence of Open Space

For the Peacemaker, there is a special opportunity in the moment of silence, the open space between what was and may be. It is to pose the question, *What are you going to do for the rest of your life?* lovingly and await the answer. This is not about offering a new life plan, or recommending the policies and procedures that will mend a broken situation. It is not about making any statement at all. It is about asking a question, for questions have the wonderful capacity to open more space. Answers almost invariably close the space down. With such a spacious environment, the innate powers of self-organization can animate the complex adaptive system which I think we all are. Who knows what the result will be, but it is bound to be different, and probably exciting. You will know that something positive is happening when you hear three little words: *I wonder if...*

Vision

For the Peacemaker, the arrival of Vision is cause for celebration. Indeed, there is really nothing to be done but celebrate, which is no small act. In celebration we honor where we have come from, those who journeyed with us, and where we are going, even if we don't have a real clue. Live it up, until the next time. For as surely as the sun rises in the morning and sets in the evening, so also will our adventures rise and fall. And once again it will be time for the Peacemaker.

A PRACTICE OF PEACE: SUMMARY

The practice, as I suggested at the start, is extraordinarily simple. Open space wherever, however, and any time you can, in order to allow the natural powers of all self-organizing systems do what they do best: create wholeness, health and harmony in themselves and with their environment. This may mean using Open Space Technology, and in certain situations the approach can be superbly effective. It may equally, and perhaps more often, mean assuming the open space mentality, that graciously spacious approach to life which starts with invitation, gathers in a circle, always remembers the Four Principles, honors the Law of Two Feet, and keeps Grief working. Such graciousness need not be reserved for special occasions, like a party dress or tuxedo hung in a closet until the time is right. It is everyday attire, for every day is a good day to engage the Practice of Peace.

And is that all there is? Of course not! Just the beginning, a practice, which becomes effective only in application. From mammoth projects to trivial moments, everything goes better in an environment of Peace. There are in fact thousands of roads we may follow on the journey.

CHAPTER VII
Many Roads to Peace

Every moment of the day provides an opportunity to create the conditions for Peace, for Peacemaking is not a special activity undertaken only in moments of intense and violent conflict. Indeed, such moments are a clear indication that we have not been doing our daily jobs as Peacemakers. For Peace itself is not the far off, someday to be realized phenomenon which we desperately seek when there seems to be no other alternative. Rather, Peace is what life is all about, every day, all the days, from the first day until the last. Just as chaos, confusion and conflict are integral elements of living, so also is the Practice of Peace, that task of enabling the conditions under which all the elements may weave themselves together, creating the fabric of life. We will never get it right. We are always on the journey, for Peace is not a destination, a final state or a frozen ideal. It is the journey itself, characterized by wholeness, health and harmony. Always moving, always changing, always exploring new ways, and therefore presenting new challenges, new insights, new opportunities. And for sure, when we reach a day where it appears that we have finally gotten it right, and all the pieces fit, we will know that the journey is over. In the meantime, there is a lot of work to do.

THE ROADS BEFORE US

This book does not have the space, nor, I am sure, do you have the patience, to explore all the possible roads to Peace. And, needless to say, I do not possess the necessary experience, knowledge and competence. My intent, therefore, will be to offer some examples from my own experience, which may be of assistance as you make your own way. This is not a cook book, for the stew of life and Peace is always a work in progress, and the chefs are infinite in number. And in the case of

Peace and Peacemaking, the old adage, "Too many cooks spoil the broth," simply does not apply.

This may be the place to offer apologies, if apologies are in order, to you my friends and colleagues who may have taken offense at what may have seemed a cavalier attitude towards the many important efforts undertaken to date in the search for Peace. Whether that be at the negotiating table, the design and implementation of the multiple facets of what might be generally called nation building and organization renewal and development, or in the less public, lower profile enterprises of "people to people" engagements. I meant no slight, indeed, I salute them all.

My concern, then and now, is not what we have been doing, but *how* we have done it. Efforts undertaken in the mode of Top Down/Command and Control may have immediate impact, even immediate positive impact (people stop shooting each other), but the longer term effect is not as promising. The reason is simple. The mode of operation is the very antithesis of Peace. The system addressed (company, county, country, region) is usually not appreciated in its full, complex diversity (all levels, all quadrants ala Ken Wilber). Chaos, confusion and conflict are eliminated if possible, rather than honored for the gifts they give, and then invited to integrate into the larger fabric. And most destructive, and therefore least effective, is the presumption that those who undertake the project actually know what they are doing, and therefore feel at liberty to impose their authority, their design, their control. All of the above may well be done with the best of altruistic intentions, but that does not change the fact that the object of their attention, that open, living, complex adaptive system is never enabled, or encouraged to do what only it can do best, heal itself.

When the attitude (mode of operation) changes from Top Down/Command and Control into what I have called "gracious spaciousness," the impact can be very different, and certainly the approach is conducted in a manner some might consider positively strange. We never work harder than we have to, we avoid fixing what is not broken, and we never delude ourselves into thinking we are in charge. Such behavior would be cause for dismissal in a number of organizations I know. But when the task is Peacemaking, I believe this is the only way to go. Therefore my suggestion is not that we stop all of the many useful interventions we have mounted in the search for Peace (education, infrastructure building, organization development, nutrition programs, and on, and on, and on…), but rather that we do them in a different way, which I think we will find to be infinitely easier, and ultimately more effective.

In what follows, I offer three examples. Only one involves the use of Open Space Technology, and the other two are definitely a matter of attitude. I do not think that these examples are unique, or that my ability is anything special. Friends and colleagues around the world have been doing the same and better, and doubtless there are an infinite number of others who are doing more who remain totally unknown to me. So what I offer is by way of example, with the hope that you and others will come forward to tell your tales, and most importantly, to engage in what I have found to be a delightful and grand experiment.

LEARNING AT THE EDGE OF THE BAY

Almost forty years ago, when I was an Associate Director in the United States Peace Corps in Liberia, I found myself in the midst of a most remarkable opportunity. At first glance it may appear to have little relationship to Peacemaking, but given the potential for conflict, massive confusion and enormous chaos, all manifested as discord, fragmentation and dis-ease, my work was cut out for me. Since this occurred almost forty years ago, Open Space Technology was not even remotely a part of the picture. I must also confess that as a 30-something year old professional with very limited experience, and less formal training, doing what I was called upon to do, there is no question that I was not working from thought through principles and practice, I simply did what seemed to be a good idea at the time.

Here was the situation. Peace Corps had recruited 150 new volunteers, all slated for duty in Liberia, West Africa as elementary school teachers. Unfortunately, there had been a small administrative slip. Absolutely no provision had been made for their training, no site selected, program developed or staff hired. This glitch was of more than incidental concern to me and my fellow Associate Directors, for these volunteers were the replacement for our current crop, all of whom were going home at the conclusion of their two year tour. Without the replacements, there would be no program and no job. To make things even more interesting, I was actually in Liberia, 5000 miles away from the United States, and the new recruits were to assemble in something less than 6 weeks.

Breaking virtually all tradition and procedure, the Home Office, Peace Corps/Washington, asked us in the field if we would accept responsibility for the training of the volunteers, and also supply the direction, which meant finding the site, creating the program, and fielding the staff. For all the reasons mentioned above, this was an offer we could scarcely refuse. For reasons I never quite understood, I was selected as one of two field officers to do the deed. It is pertinent to note that I was not an elementary school teacher, nor had I ever had any training as such. My only exposure to the arcane art of educating juveniles came though the eyes of my current volunteers, who were doing just that. It was starting to look like a wonderful case of the blind leading the blind.

There are cases, however, where ignorance can be a positive advantage. In this particular situation I felt that what I lacked in knowledge (answers) I more than made up for with questions. Not only my own, but also those of my volunteers. Perhaps it is my own perverse nature, but it had been my experience that having the right (i.e., pertinent, relevant) questions to be infinitely more satisfying and useful than all the answers in the world. And it seemed that in most training programs the participants were buried in answers to questions they never asked and/or didn't understand. The net effect was rote retention of answers with little understanding of their application. From this minimal base came my approach: Find/create an environment in which the questions are obvious, the space is sufficient for exploration, and resources (albeit minimal) are available for resolution.

I felt certain that the richest resource would be the volunteer/ trainees themselves. Peace Corps volunteers are a special breed. Prerequisite to their selection is a college degree and/or some useful and demonstrated life skill or trade. They are signing on for two years' hard work in non-tourist destinations, with people who typically have not known the finer things of life. All this for little pay, except for the satisfaction of meeting a difficult challenge, and the added self knowledge and worldly experience that comes with it. That of course is priceless. In any event, commitment, dedication, motivation, innovation, and just plain guts can all be pretty well assumed. If we could just add a few things like books, or people expert in such things as Math/science, lesson planning, classroom management, educational materials, and a few others pertinent to the realm of the elementary school in a third world environment, the next step would be a simple one. Just open the space, get out of the way, and let the volunteers get to work, which I was sure they would do if they only knew what the work was. What are the questions?

Questions can be of an intellectual sort, but the best ones I've found were those messy existential monsters that just pop out of daily experience, if you have the experience. At this point the site became critical. It turned out that Peace Corps maintained a training facility on the Island of St. Thomas in the U.S. Virgin Islands. And best of all it was available for the time period required. A tad on the rustic side (which was good), it occupied a physical space that simply took our breath away. Perched on rolling hills overlooking the Caribbean, with Megan's Bay at our feet, the site was incredible. But what lay around it was better: The Virgin Island School System. Multiple elementary schools catering to a population of largely poor, Black children, all lodged in a Caribbean culture which had a certain uniqueness, but also a deep rootedness in Africa. And they were ready and willing to play. A marvelous school superintendent made a light-speed decision (for school systems) to welcome our volunteers, exact program to be determined as we went along.

Six weeks from the day it all began we were ready to open the doors for business. The program could begin, if you could call it a program. And official Peace Corps/Washington was having a terribly difficult time swallowing that designation.

Cables and phone calls came in abundance: what were we going to do, when were we going to do it, to what specific end and result, and how, pray tell, did we propose to evaluate the effort?

My answers were scarcely comforting. In truth I didn't have a clue regarding the particulars. But I had great faith in the volunteers, confidence that the appropriate questions would be raised in a potent and clear fashion, and reasonable comfort in the several content experts who had agreed to join the adventure, plus the books and other literature they provided. As for the rest, we did have telephones, cable service (no faxes or Internet in those days), and libraries on the island, so something would work out. Regarding the detail of "The Program," I knew only when we would start, when we would end, and not much more. As for evaluation, that would be clear, precise and effective. If the volunteers could effectively teach kids when they arrived in Liberia, and managed to do so over the course of their two year tour, the program was a success. If otherwise, it was not.

To say that officialdom was nervous puts the situation rather mildly. Some people actually suggested that I be relieved of my duties, and I invited them to do that. They asked for assurances, and I promised that we would do the program on time, under budget, and that the volunteers who went to the field would serve with distinction. In the event that some or all of that did not occur, I took full responsibility, which frankly didn't make my interrogators feel much better. And in the interim, I asked that they not second guess me—just keep the space open.

Oh yes, there was also the matter of Selection (with a capitol S). At the time, Peace Corps had a massive final selection procedure which was to take place at the conclusion of the training program. Psychologists in profusion would descend on the camp and conduct endless reviews with groups, individuals, and staff of the program. Then, usually through a very long night, they made The Decision. The Fortunates and the Unfortunates were informed on the following morning. I had never been a part of one of these inquisitions, but I had seen the results in the field. In terms of eliminating incompetents and dilettantes, it didn't seem to have much effect. But the level of trauma induced by the whole affair was bitter and embittering. And so my final outrage, no Selection. If a volunteer wanted to go, baring obvious illegal or immoral activities, he or she would go. I felt our responsibility was to make the program realistic. The volunteers must decide if they really wanted to spend two years in a bush village with little pay and minimal creature comforts, teaching kids. And so we began.

Ninety-five trainees (the balance went off to a different site) showed up at beautiful Megan's Bay in time for dinner. The next morning we went to work. Truthfully, we had a little more of a planned program than I have indicated, but not much. On the first day, we covered the necessary administrative detail, Peace Corps procedures and expectations. On the second day, several of my African friends talked about their land, their hopes and their dreams. Nothing too detailed, just a rich, raw, humorous, sad taste. At the end of the day, one of the Africans pointed East into the gathering evening. He said, "Africa is that way. We'll meet you there."

On the morning of the third day things began in earnest. A string of school buses greeted the volunteers as they left breakfast, and took them all to the several elementary schools of the V.I. System. Upon arrival they were welcomed by the marvelous teachers who had agreed to be the learning guides for the next six weeks: one teacher, one volunteer, one classroom, and a simple scheme. For the first week the volunteer was expected only to look and listen closely, maybe help at juice and cracker time, but nothing more. In the second week, the volunteer would be responsible for one hour of classroom instruction every day. The third week, two hours, and so on until the sixth week, when these new volunteers would take over the whole enchilada with the teacher as observer and coach.

When the school day ended, the buses returned the volunteers to the camp, and the afternoons and evenings, with minor exceptions, were pure open space. We did point out that potentially useful resources were available in the library and in the persons of the several "experts" who had joined us. To make things a little easier we randomly assigned volunteers to groups of roughly ten with a returned Peace Corps volunteer as sort of combination den mother and pack leader. If a volunteer didn't like their group, they were at full liberty to find another. However, putting it all together was 100% up to them.

Did we have chaos, confusion and conflict? You bet! And it was wonderful. But mostly what we had was learning at a profound, painful, joyful level. Every day, the relevant questions appeared in the faces of the 30+ kids gathered in the classroom. Not some academic abstraction neatly described in a book on educational methods, but the real thing: noisy, dirty, clean, smiling, sulking, well-behaved, and totally out of control. It was all there, and how do you manage? What do you teach?

Skeptics had indicated prior to the inception of the program that it was highly likely that the volunteers would discover the beach at Megan's Bay, and never leave. Nothing could have been further from the truth. Those volunteers were so excited, highly motivated and desperate to learn—a desperation born of the sure and certain knowledge that the next morning there would be 30+ kids in their face for whom they were responsible. The ambient energy was overwhelming to the point that my "invited experts" took on a haggard look as their sessions, formal and informal, stretched into the midnight hours. There were endless peer teaching gatherings as volunteers assisted volunteers, and collectively built the common knowledge and practice. If this was supposed to be a day at the beach, we never quite got there.

Actually, by the end of the third week, I was becoming seriously concerned about folks. The level of intense effort was such that I felt major burn out was a distinct possibility. I knew I could never get them to just stop and go to the beach, but a pause and change in direction might help.

In the very nick of time a school holiday appeared on the horizon, and we canceled what little program we had. All hands assembled after breakfast and I invited them to go on a Treasure Hunt of a rather different sort. I tore out sections of the National Liberian Curriculum, and passed them out to the several volunteer groups, one page per group. The instructions were, find the essential educational materials in order to teach the subject matter on your page. You may go anywhere on the island, beg, borrow, or steal as necessary, understanding that if you end in jail I cannot help. And they were off.

To this day, I don't have a clue where they went, or what they did. But I do know that in the evening upon their return, the place was humming. When you invite a group of young people to go out on what almost literally turned out to be a wild goose chase, the results can be surprising. For a unit on Animal Husbandry (or something like that) the volunteers returned with several chickens, a goat and a donkey (no geese). And also the farmer, who insisted that he come along. For a unit on Use of the Library, the enterprising volunteers showed up with two live librarians. And so it went.

After dinner, which was extended because everybody also had to prepare their lessons which they would "teach" to their peers, the show began. Something between a wild cabaret and a serious seminar, it went on for hours, but nobody seemed to mind. Fortunately the next day was a Saturday, so a lengthy sleep-in was possible, and of course we did (finally) get to the beach.

The program ended several weeks later, and the volunteers went to Africa. We did actually convene a Selection Board, because it seemed that somebody had to sign something saying everybody could go. But it was mercifully short, and followed by a humongous party to which all the teachers from the schools and their significant others were invited, 300 people who had become friends and colleagues. A steel band appeared miraculously, and I went to bed long before the final guest departed.

My tour with Peace Corps ended shortly after the volunteers arrived in Liberia so I cannot provide any evaluation from personal experience. However, my colleagues (the other Associate Directors) told me that the attrition rate (volunteers being sent home, or choosing to leave) was less than average, although a few did go. As for performance in the field, it was certainly up to par, with the major plus being that the normal period of adjustment was radically reduced. Those volunteers hit the ground running. Dealing with an obstreperous bunch of youngsters was not a strange experience, and volunteer self reliance was at an all time high.

My purpose in telling this tale is to give some flesh and blood to the notion that it is quite possible to approach a very standard activity (training/education) in a very different way to enable the complex adaptive system, which the volunteers quickly became, to function at high levels of effectiveness with minimal support and structure. Other Peace Corps programs at the time, and indeed most such programs presently (Peace Corps or not), were/are scheduled down to the minute, with the harried program director desperately trying to maintain control. I was never in control, and I knew it. I would be lying were I to suggest that my approach grew out of a deep understanding of the process of self-organization. Truthfully, I had never heard of such a thing, and in fact I was only doing what seemed to be a good idea at the time. I muddled through.

Some might see the effort as a lucky, aberrant phenomenon, but I think the truth of the matter is that we all muddle through, and the very fact that I had no real control from the beginning, due to force of circumstances—and knew it—was a positive advantage. Knowing what I know now, I would actually choose this way, but at the time it seemed the only thing to do. All of which makes the point, I think, that what might seem aberrant and surprising was actually quite predictable. The fact that I didn't have a clue what I was doing only made the adventure a more interesting natural experiment. Given our present knowledge about self-organizing systems, what happened was probably the only thing that could have, and should not have come as a surprise.

This begs the question, was this Peacemaking? My answer would be an unqualified yes. We surely had an abundance of chaos, confusion and conflict which at every moment threatened to dissolve into monumental masses of discord, fragmentation and dis-ease. Every time I attempted to seize the bull by the horns and render order out of chaos (gain control) it only got worse. Had I been successful, my wonderfully motivated, creative volunteers would have probably toed the line, but the cost would have been enormous, and revolt was not impossible. Actually, there are many stories of palace coups being staged in training programs to the point that some trainers found themselves predicting and expecting such a coup, which then necessitated endless sessions in which the ambient feelings were "processed." We never had such a moment, or more precisely every time one approached we instinctively opened more space, and the nascent conflict resolved itself with a marvelous release of creative energy. And best of all, it happened all by itself. The dynamic equilibrium of the group restored itself, and we got on with the business of preparing young men and women for a challenging task. So was this Peacemaking? Yes, and over the course of our six weeks together we experienced that Peace as a constantly unfolding journey of exploration. Highs and lows, pitfalls and pinnacles all made their appearance, but on the whole, indeed most of the time, it all just flowed. And that is what I would call real Peace.

THE PINK PANTHER RALLY

Far removed from the world of Peace Corps is the corporate domain. Indeed Peace Corps volunteers, along with many other young people in the 1960s and now, viewed the corporate world as a hostile, strange, malevolent environment populated by regimented souls in grey suits. It was the citadel of power and control where tightly managed engines of efficiency did their thing. The thought of Peace and Peacemaking in such a place would not occur, for who would suspect that such a human need could surface in that paragon of efficiency and monument to the bottom line? It turns out, of course, that corporations are human too, and more than occasionally things fall apart in a welter of discord, fragmentation and dis-ease. The causes are multiple, ranging from drastic changes in the external environment to self-inflicted wounds. In the 1980s, Owens Corning Fiberglas (OCF) found itself victim of all of the above.

OCF was reputed to be one of the best managed corporations in the U.S., at least that is what *Fortune Magazine* found for several years running. As the inventor and major manufacturer of fiberglass they had created and dominated their market. In the early 1970s, during the oil crunch which drove up costs, particularly heating costs, householders were desperate for good insulation, which created such demand that OCF virtually stopped all sales efforts, and moved to some form of allocation. In short, business was very good. By the early '80s they were a four billion dollar a year operation with lots of cash in the bank. And that was a problem, for that was the time of the corporate raiders.

One such "raider" was the owner of a lumber yard chain on the West Coast, and also a longtime customer of OCF. But he had larger things on his mind and initiated a hostile takeover bid. The prize was all that cash in the bank, and he tried to convince his fellow stockholders to sell out in the belief that the spare cash should be distributed to worthy stockholders and a new management installed. He almost succeeded, but not quite. Through Herculean effort, existing management sold assets, cut deals, radically downsized to save costs (increase shareholder return), and emerged victorious. But the victory was almost Pyrrhic. The once proud corporation had been cut in half, virtually overnight. A four billion dollar a year corporation was now just a shade over two, and in many ways that was the least of the pain. Many people had lost their jobs, and those who remained feared (with real justification) that they too were on the short list for termination. Not a happy place, made all the more unhappy by virtue of the fact that in the past their ample resources had enabled OCF to solve problems and build the business with a massive (and expensive) workforce. They now had all the problems, and all the needs, with only a fraction of the people they were accustomed to.

Last, but by no means least, those who remained had become very comfortable with what was known as the OCF Way, which meant endless, detailed procedures for every task and problem, all carefully controlled by well trained managers. The net result was a well ordered, tightly controlled machine which did not tolerate deviation. Or put another way, virtually eliminated innovation. Nobody would ever publicly say as much, but new ideas and approaches were definitely suspect, and those who espoused such things were considered more than a little odd, if not dangerous, a fact which became clear in a little aphorism which became a (secret) part of the local mythology. It was said that the CEO always said, "Never turn the asylum over to the inmates." The asylum was of course the company, and the inmates the employees. Under such conditions, it is little wonder that innovation was virtually absent, and taking personal responsibility for bold initiatives was avoided. Definitely not a happy place, and desperately in need of Peace in the fullest sense of my use of the word: The restoration of wholeness, health and harmony.

As it happened, I had been retained by the company with the hope that I might be of some assistance. The central issue was clear, get the place moving. Concretely this meant restoring levels of confidence, to say nothing of personal respect, encouraging and supporting innovation, and more importantly, rebuilding a sense of responsibility for actions taken, whether they resulted in success or failure. The local myth about The Asylum had only a wispy relationship to historical fact. I never heard the CEO say such a thing, nor could I ever find anyone who had. But none of that changed the power of the myth. It was everywhere and whatever it may have lacked in historical validity, it surely made up for the present currency. Putting it simply, a lot of the folks felt like inmates in an asylum. This feeling alone was probably sufficient to kill off whatever responsible innovation still may have lurked on the premises.

Obviously, there is a number of what might be termed "standard approaches" to the kinds of issues faced by OCF. Training programs designed to enhance innovation and creativity, organizational redesign, to improve the environment, and possibly no small amount of coaching and personal therapy for those in need. There were two problems with all of these approaches. Typically, they required a lot of time and no small amount of money, neither of which was abundantly available.

There was also a *Catch 22,*[31] or maybe it was the chicken and egg problem we previously encountered. Precisely the people who must create this new environment of innovation, creativity and responsibility were exactly the ones who were deficient in all three. So where did you start?

Today I would answer we just open some space and allow the good old self-organizing system (OCF) to catch its breath and return to operations, in the course of which innovation, creativity, responsibility as well as personal respect and dignity would all show up. Or they wouldn't, in which case it would be clear that no matter how long the artificial respiration might be carried out, the patient was terminal. It really wouldn't make much difference what the theme of the Open Space was, so long as people truly cared about it. Everything else would take care of itself. Open Space Technology, however, did not exist, but everything else was in place. We only had to find it.

"It" was any latent spark of creativity and innovation located anywhere in the system which might be fanned into a flame given the air and the space. It needn't be a high level thing, or a big thing, just any thing or person. In fact it would be best if "it" appeared small, powerless and inconsequential for then, once alight it would be clear that great things can come in small packages. Or in slightly different terms, it would demonstrate that one did not need action by the board, personal commitment from the CEO, and massive amounts of money and planning. Renewal could start anywhere with anyone.

---

[31] For those who may not remember, "a Catch 22" was the "damned if you do and damned if you don't" sort of thing, which originated in a wonderful novel by Joseph Heller titled *Catch 22.*

"It" fell right into our hands. During a presentation I was making of my findings to date, I mentioned that the fatigue and stress levels were at an all time high, and even though obvious progress was being made to strengthen the balance sheet, and to manufacture and move product, the people I was talking to were just about at the end of their string. Facetiously, I suggested that it might be the right time to call a break and have a party which would celebrate the progress to date, and all those who had made it possible, while simultaneously sounding a clarion call for renewed effort.

I really was joking, but to my surprise two young women, almost simultaneously, raised their hand and said, "We'll do it!" There *it* was in the persons of Sharon Peters, an executive secretary, and Tamara Kristen, a junior accountant. The precious flame, and best of all it was two young women, who in the massively male dominated, pin striped, culture of OCF constituted the epitome of powerlessness. But there was no doubting their commitment and enthusiasm. Throwing caution to the wind, I said, "Great! What can we do to help?" And wisely they said, "We'll let you know." The meeting adjourned.

We did in fact have a secret weapon in place in the person of my friend and colleague at OCF, John Zaloudek. John was a very bright and sensitive executive who had been around long enough to have gained the respect and trust of most of the senior people. As the meeting ended and the two women dashed off to do whatever they were going to do, John and I had a short huddle. To call it a planning session would be a vast overstatement. It was apparent to both of us that for the enterprise to have any chance of success, Tamara and Sharon needed a little cover, not so much that they felt patronized or restricted, but sufficient to keep the natural bureaucratic antibodies of the corporation at a distance, at least until the effort took on a life of its own. In a word, John became the chief space holder, the very embodiment of gracious spaciousness, who did little, always used what was freely available (or could be begged, borrowed or stolen), and never deluded himself into thinking he was in charge.

I confess at this point the details of the timing and events are lost to me. In broad brush, however, it seemed that the two women started with the most powerful tool in their possession, the telephone. This instantaneously gave them access to the (I think) most powerful aspect of the corporation, the informal organization, which they knew intimately. After all, this was the "place" where they conducted business everyday to accomplish essential tasks that otherwise were beyond their reach. As the story has it, within 48 hours they had commitments from 30+ people to come to a meeting several days hence where The Plan would be hatched. It is doubtful that the CEO himself could have cleared the calendar of 30+ busy people on such short notice, but the women did it.

When the meeting convened there was no agenda or observable chair person. The folks just talked. In short order the party idea transformed into a rally to be known as the Pink Pride Rally in honor of the Pink Panther, the mascot and logo of OCF, and the size of the event swelled from something small to include potentially a cast of thousands. Needs were identified, responsibility accepted, and it was over—or just beginning.

The details of what happened next were largely hidden from view, although they quickly became part of a growing story which sounded infinitely better than being an inmate at an asylum. To the best of my knowledge, there was never a budget, or never one that anyone could find. Nobody ever asked permission to hold the rally, and none was given. In fact the two women decided that they would simply invite the CEO to attend, and they did. Of course there were bumps along the way, many of which my friend John had no small part in smoothing out.

One of these bumps came from the Director of Corporate Communications who thought that the whole affair belonged in his shop, and was terribly concerned that things would get out of control—bad press and such. He apparently made appeals to the CEO and also the Board, I think, and for a moment it looked as if the growing flame was about ready to flame out. But John came to the rescue, not by solving the problem, but by convincing the communications executive that he at least ought to meet with the women before he pulled the plug. Except for some introductions, I don't think John said a thing. Tamara and Sharon did it all, and there was a lot to be done. Sharp, pointed questions were asked in abundance, and with great patience, and obvious understanding, the women delivered the answers until the nervous executive threw his hands in the air and said, "This is wonderful. How can I help you?" So much for the problem.

When the great day arrived, just six short weeks after my facetious remark about a party, it all unfolded. Something like a thousand people gathered in the public square of Toledo, Ohio decked out in pink T shirts emblazoned with a naughty pink panther, drank pink lemonade, were serenaded by a band, listened to a few short speeches. They were surrounded by several trailer trucks full of old sales exhibits that made the place OCF, all under a large banner with huge letters that said THANK YOU EVERYBODY. Not bad for two young women with no budget, no permission, no plan, no organizational structure, and little status as their corporate colleagues might have seen it.

Of course, there were a few skeptics who said, well, that was just a party. But most people knew it was a lot more. In place of the old story of being inmates in an asylum, there was a new story all about risk taking, innovation, and accomplishing what many thought would be impossible. And everybody had to believe it because they had all been a part of it. For the number crunchers there were even some interesting figures. OCF, like many corporations in the building business, often threw large parties for their customers, who were largely contractors, lumberyards and the like. These parties might only entertain 400–500 people but their cost could exceed $1,000,000 and take over a year to plan. Against that background throwing a bash for a thousand folks, with no budget, and created in 6 weeks, looked very good.

It is reasonable to ask whether all the corporate problems were solved, and of course the answer is no. But we did make a significant start, creating a foothold that was leveraged, but that is another, and much longer tale. It may also be important to point out that my contribution, other than the initial off-hand comment was essentially zero. Unless you count a great deal of quiet cheerleading from hundreds of miles away. I didn't even have the opportunity to go to the rally itself.

The real heroes of this tale were obviously Tamara and Sharon, and of course, John Zaloudek. I mentioned previously that I found the fact that the "leaders" were young women was significant, and surprising, in the male dominated culture of OCF. The significance, at a superficial level, appears in their powerlessness, or at least presumed powerlessness. Having neither rank nor tenure, these two were clearly the least likely to bring such a venture to fruition, or so the conventional thinking might have been. Yet, when perceived as an exercise of self-organization they were clearly the perfect choice. Intuitively (or at least I think it was intuitively), they knew and practiced what I have described as the essential elements of a practice of Peace, beginning with invitation. Since they had no power to command, they could only invite, which insured that those who came, came because they wanted to— even the CEO. And by this act of invitation they conferred respect and dignity on those who joined, not as an award given from some all powerful position, but rather as gift of appreciation and acknowledgment. For those who perceived themselves as inmates in an asylum, this was precious.

When it came to *passion and responsibility* this remarkable pair obviously walked their talk, thereby becoming a model for all the rest. This was leadership at its finest, so far as I am concerned. Indeed, I have found that whenever you encounter the combination of passion and responsibility; powerful, effective leadership seems to appear virtually instantaneously. Genuine leadership is rarely, if ever, a function of title, position and authority. Indeed one may have all of those, and absent passion and responsibility, not very much gets done.[32]

The Four Principles showed up constantly. Obviously, *whoever came were the right people* as demonstrated by the fact that despite all odds, it worked. What happened with that group was not a function of some preconceived master plan, it grew organically as people explored their Now, making it

---

[32] For more on Leadership in a non-command and control mode, you might consult my book, *The Spirit of Leadership,* Berrett-Koehler, 1999.

bigger—a wonderful demonstration of the second principle, *Whatever happens is the only thing that could have.* And of course, *Whenever it started was the right time.* This event never held a space on the corporate calendar, it happened when it happened. Eventually, of course, a date for the event was designated, and on that date the people assembled, but not at the time or place they expected. A part of the tale I neglected to tell concerned the appearance of a massive thunderstorm just as the festivities were supposed to get under way. It could have been disaster, but in a miraculously short time the whole thing was moved from the Town Square to the municipal parking garage. That means everything—a lot of people, a band, trailer trucks full of exhibits, T-shirts, lemonade, a logistical feat of some magnitude, all done without a plan. When it started, it was indeed the right time. Lastly, *when it was over, it was over.* To be sure there were a few celebrations to celebrate the celebration, but people went right back to work, rebuilding OCF. To be sure, some went back as unhappy as they came, but others came to know what no argument could ever convince them of, their own dignity and self-worth.

The fact that the leadership of this adventure was manifest in the passion and responsibility of two young women is significant in another and possibly deeper way. I have noticed over the years as I work with Open Space Technology, and particularly training people to use it, that women definitely get it. Not all women, nor are men excluded, but more often than not it is the women who find their way first. There is a fair amount in the feminist literature that speaks of The Woman's Way, and this may be an example of it. I doubt that the appreciation of the self-organizing system, and the ability to work comfortably within it, is a gender-specific trait, at least I hope not. On my side is the fact men can do just as well, even when they are quite unconscious of what they are doing. A case in point was my friend John Zaloudek, who was for me a model of gracious spaciousness. So there is hope for the male of the species, and with some help and practice everybody seems to do better, and in fact get along just fine.

THE YWCA OF USA

My final example includes the use of Open Space Technology as an initiatory part of the process. It should be quite clear by now that the use of OST is by no means obligatory if only because the essential mechanisms in play preexist OST by millennia. There is a certain advantage, however, when the powers of self-organization are utilized consciously and intentionally in the Practice of Peace.

For those of you who don't know, the YWCA (Young Women's Christian Association) is an old and honorable institution, at least by U.S. standards. It was founded shortly after the turn of the last century at a time when women, particularly young women, were subjected to what can only be called excessive domination and suppression. They could not vote, few could take advantage of education, particularly at higher levels, and their opportunities for gainful employment were constrained, to say the least. For the most part, it was expected that they marry, raise children, and be content with their lot, and certainly never challenge the dominant male authority. Not a happy situation, and scarcely peaceful, although on the surface it appeared that all was right with the world, at least the male world.

The YWCA came into existence to provide a safe place for the nurture and growth of young women, with the hope and expectation that they might assume their rightful place in society as fully respected individuals and human beings. For more than 100 years the YW, as many called it, pursued its mission with success.

Over the years, and particularly in later years, signs of institutional hardening of the arteries became inescapable. Layers of bureaucracy and mountains of procedures stifled creative enterprise. Good things continued to happen, but it was a battle all the way. At the core of this battle was a rancorous dispute between the national board and the multiple local agencies. This board was actually the creation of the local groups in an effort to coordinate and expand their influence. But as often is the way of such things, the board came to see itself as being in charge, no longer the servant of the local organizations, but their master, or I suppose mistress would be more appropriate. The effect was disastrous as more energy was devoted to running the bureaucracy and fighting its battles than to providing support to their clients, the young women of America. Not only was it unpleasant, it was down right destructive, which might give pause to those who would believe that women are somehow immune to some of the nastier behaviors common to humanity.

The looming situation was duly noted, and steps were taken to make changes, which always seemed to involve some sort of major study, followed by a report which found its place next to the earlier reports in the institutional archives. The situation remained unchanged, or got worse.

A few years ago, a small group, composed largely of the leaders of local organizations, and led by members of the National Association of YWCA Executives, basically said, Enough is enough! Something seriously has to change even though we can't say exactly what, or how. This marked the birth of what came to be known as, The Change Initiative, which had no official standing and few resources, but was ready to go to work. There seemed to be an additional point of consensus: Whatever else happened, there would not be another study.

How I became involved in all this remains a mystery to this day, at least to me. However, I did receive a call from Myrna Deckert, chairperson of The Change Initiative, and a most remarkable woman. She briefly explained the situation and invited me to write a proposal to fix it. I responded by saying (as gently as I could) that I did not do proposals. Being the lady that she was, she didn't miss a beat and replied. "Well if you were to write a proposal, what would you say?" My answer was very short and simple: Open Space.

To be honest, I must confess that I did write a proposal in order to satisfy the bureaucratic requirements, but it said scarcely more than I had at the start. Open Space. And that is exactly what we did.

Five hundred women from all over the United States, representing every conceivable aspect of the YWCA, assembled in Dallas. Young women who had been members but for a short time, veterans, staff, board members—they all came. We met in a low-ceilinged convention hall, which had an additional problem in that its many pillars made it impossible to get a straight view of anything from anywhere. The space was less than desirable, but nobody seemed to care. They were all present, all ready, and nobody had a clue where we were headed. The invitation had been circumspect, basically saying little more than that a change was needed, and Dallas was the place to start.

It would actually be a gross error to suggest that those in attendance had no idea of what should be done, but it was quickly obvious that their individual prescriptions were as various and conflicted as the polyglot of people themselves. All wonderful, all committed, all caring, and all (it seemed) in different ways. And so we began, 500 women and me.

As an Open Space, it was hardly remarkable. Issues were raised, discussions engaged, tears were shed, tempers flared, hugs were administered, and laughter bubbled here and there. Highs and lows came and went—from tense confrontation to creative problem solving, nonstop for two days. On the morning of the third day, out of something like 100 issues raised, some 10 or 11 topped the rest based on the group's prioritization. None of the remainder were lost, and most were converged with the top rankers. Action plans were sketched out, and responsibility assumed for their implementation. Shortly before noon we sat in a silent circle and then the participants shared their experience and their feelings.

It quickly became apparent that for all of the concrete accomplishments (new plans made, old approaches laid to one side) the signal accomplishment was infinitely more profound: Peace. The comments of the participants and the testimony of the atmosphere all spoke to a radical change in being. Chaos, confusion and conflict continued to exist, but no longer were they purely destructive forces. For the YWCA, the chaos created by a changing membership, world and needs opened new possibilities for services, which were then recognized. Confusion mellowed strongly held, dogmatic positions so that new approaches could find acceptance. And conflict provided the needed abrasion to sharpen thinking and hone effective action. For the moment, and in that moment, they knew Peace as organizational integrity (wholeness), reduction of stress and strain (health), and the multiple disparate pieces worked together (harmony). And they sang. I don't remember the words, and it was probably more than one song, but they honored the past and welcomed the future. Hugs, tears, and laughter broke out in profusion, for the people had become, for the moment, the vision they sought. It remained to be seen if that vision could be sustained. And I don't think it escaped anybody that they had done it all by themselves, and nobody was in charge—certainly not me.

As I have said, the Open Space in Dallas was by no means remarkable as Open Spaces go. What happened there had happened thousands of times previously. No news. But the reason I offer it as an example is because of what happened afterwards. It could have been the case that the 500 women would have gone home and simply taken up where they had left off with the various battles, bureaucratic and personal. Back to business as usual. Truth to tell, they never quite could go back, for they would always know that a different way was available. And the basis of their knowledge was that bedrock of all firm knowledge: experience. They had been in a different space, encountered different behaviors, felt together in a very different way. If they had chosen to go back to the way things were, they would have been doubly damned. Not only would it have been just as uncomfortable and non-productive as always, but they would have been haunted with a memory of a vision glimpsed and squandered. While they certainly could have backslid their way to misery and frustration, they didn't, and that is the rest, and best part, of the tale.

Immediately after the conclusion of the gathering in Dallas the several action teams went to work, gathering more information, building constituencies, creating plans and making it happen. This effort was led by Audrey Peoples and her Transition Team, which for two years guided the intense activity, all powered by energized, committed and focused people. Large potholes appeared in the road which had to be filled, or detoured, but the movement muddled through. Every skill that anybody had ever learned was put to work, legal, personal, organizational, and I am sure, therapeutic. And there was also a new skill that Myrna and her close colleagues had learned in Dallas that they continued to use when they got home. When in doubt, conflict or confusion, open space. It needn't be a formally convened Open Space event, just remember the essentials. Start with an invitation, create a circle, remember the Four Principles, and always observe the Law of Two Feet. And don't forget passion and responsibility. Every communication I received from Myrna, and particularly those that were also going to her colleagues, held the phrase somewhere: Keep the Space Open. If *Keep the Powder Dry* was a rallying cry for the American Revolution, *Keep The Space Open* seemed to have a similar effect for the good women of the YWCA.

Sometime earlier this year, under the leadership of Christine Dalley, all the pieces came together, and in a formal gathering the Young Women's Christian Association adopted a new constitution, bylaws and organizational form which gave needed autonomy, supported by accountability, to the local organizations. Provision was also made for their common voice to be heard at a national level in support of their mission of enriching the lives of young women. I am sure nobody feels that the Kingdom of God has arrived, nor that different times with different needs will never demand new forms and approaches. And when those times appear, they already know the first step. Open Space. And next time I'm sure they will have no need of me—with or without a proposal.

MANY ROADS TO PEACE

There are indeed many roads to Peace, and in presenting these three small examples, I have hardly begun to name them all. In fact all of the multiple activities that we as humans have invented to make our lives more peaceful can, and do, have positive effect, and none should be overlooked. We desperately require skilled negotiators who are willing to sit the long hours at Peace tables around the world working out effective agreements. And programs of all sorts designed to create an environment for Peace are no less critical. Education Programs to nurture hungry minds with the necessary tools to feed hungry bellies; Economic Development Programs so that the cycles of dependence are broken, and people everywhere come to know the dignity and pride that arrives with self-sufficiency; Infrastructure development programs creating the highways and byways that Peace may travel on. All these and many more are essential, but none is sufficient individually, nor are they sufficient in their totality. At the end of the day, the complexity of our enterprise, and the speed of its change and evolution overwhelm our best efforts through unintended consequences, and fixes that fix the immediate problem, but create multiple new ones. I do not feel, nor do I think others should feel, a sense of shame and inadequacy in acknowledging our limitations when it becomes very clear that our best efforts, no matter how much improved, or how often we try come up short. *What* we have been doing is marvelous, and we need to do more and better. However, we may wish to look at the *How.*

If our many efforts are conducted without the benefit of what I believe to be the greatest power at our disposal, the power of self-organization, we are truly working with one hand tied behind our backs—or maybe both hands and our feet as well. When we limit ourselves in such a fashion it is no wonder that we inevitably seem to come up short. Of course, the inherent power of any old complex adaptive systems does not disappear simply because we are unable to see it, or refuse to acknowledge its presence and potency. In fact I rather suspect that in those instances where our efforts meet with success, that success is largely attributable to the unseen and unacknowledged power in our midst. Simply put, we muddle through.

In my mind, however, simply muddling through is no longer necessary, or acceptable. We have the knowledge and we have the applications; at least we have made a useful beginning. Through the work of many fine minds, Kaufmann, Gell-Mann, Prigogine, and many, many more, we can now name that wonderful creature, The Complex Adaptive System, which seemingly lies at the core of each of us individually, and all of us collectively, as well as of the cosmos itself. As each day passes we learn more about the strange and wonderful behavior of this power resident in the core of everything. And through the gifts of two martinis, in a totally fortuitous fashion, we have a useful application, a way to apply this power for our needs. Open Space Technology, for all of its simplicity—and maybe because of its simplicity—works, even though many can't believe that it does. As an ongoing natural experiment lasting over seventeen years, with thousands of iterations in multiple spaces and places, it would seem that the Beta Tests are in. We are well past the experimental stage, although of course the experiment will always continue.

Given the knowledge and the means of application, all combined with a large and growing global experience, it remains only to put it all to work in the service of Peace. Doing less, or worse yet, doing nothing, seems to me to be the height of irresponsibility. Employing this knowledge and practice in a large and concerted fashion by no means requires that we jettison all of our prior efforts. For *what* we have been doing may well be superb. However, we have an opportunity to take a good, long, hard look at the *how*.

A colleague of mine once remarked, "Everything seems to go better with Open Space." His comment closely paralleled that from another friend who said, "I think I finally understand Open Space. It is the WD-40[33] of group work. One shot will loosen up just about anything." Facetious comments to be sure, but reflective of a large and growing body of experience. Human enterprise, undertaken in open space—whether that be a formal application of Open Space Technology, or (and more likely) the result of what we have called somewhat lamely, the Open Space Mentality—just seems to work better. No guarantees of course, but the probability of success appears to be enhanced. Given the stakes of the moment in our less than peaceful world, any margin for success can be very useful, no matter how small. It is certainly worth a try.

Trying would mean doing what we have always been doing in an "open space way." If our mission is to mount a major education program for the benefit of those in need somewhere in the world, open space. Invite those who care—and that could be potential students, parents, local officials, current teachers, outside experts, anybody—to come together in the

---

[33] WD-40 is a marvelous solvent found in most mechanics' tool chests. It works wonders with rusty bolts and cranky machinery.

initiation of the process of self-organization which will be the creative engine for all that follows. None of this can be a replacement for good curriculum, well trained teachers, educational materials, motivated students, and the funds to support it all. But the power of self-organization can transform the usual chaos, confusion and conflict into a flowing enterprise, characterized by wholeness, health and harmony, Peace. And should the toxins produced as the process rolls out become lethal—and they certainly will—make sure that grief is doing its job. Old ways and old practices will have to give way, and they will not do so without a struggle. Letting go of what has been can be very painful for those involved. After all it is through these ways and practices that they have defined their lives and judged their professional competence. When the pain of ending becomes intense, it is not unlikely that a great new project will come to a halt. Time and space must be provided for the healing power of Griefwork. And when things get sticky, or even stuck, open more space. Or best of all, keep the space open. Never work harder than you have to, don't fix it if it ain't broke, and never, ever, ever delude yourself into thinking you are in charge.

CHAPTER VIII
Preparation for Peacemaking

It may seem odd to take up the business of preparation for Peacemaking at the end of the book. But it is only now that you have available, what at least I think are, the critical skills and processes involved, combined with a sense of the demands and the cost. So now we may raise the question, How do we prepare ourselves for such an undertaking?

Unlike many other activities in our life, Peacemaking is less about acquiring new skills and methods than applying those we already possess in some new and more intentional ways. To be sure, our performance improves with practice, but the critical pieces for our endeavor are already hardwired into our being. The underlying process of self-organization will continue to operate as it has for millennia, regardless of our efforts, and Griefwork does its job without our invention, or intervention. In a word, every human being on the face of the planet comes equipped with the essential tools. It remains only to use them.

It is not my intent to downplay the needed effort required for the effective use of these tools. Developing a conceptual base from which to understand the operations of Complex Adaptive Systems, as well as the vital functions of Griefwork are more than useful. But if ever there were a case where theory without practice is useless, Peacemaking is that case. Indeed it can turn out that too much knowledge is a very bad thing. Should we find ourselves so immersed in the details of mechanisms and operations that we fail to do the needed work, there is obviously little gained. Even worse, if we were ever to conclude that we knew enough to actually know what we are doing, we might find ourselves tempted by that most egregious of sins, thinking we were in charge. In this case if a little knowledge were dangerous, complete knowledge would be disastrous.

Even in the case of Open Space Technology, where there is an obvious and definite methodology, endless training and "seeking to get it right" is a total waste of time, if we never get on with the business of opening space. I firmly believe that anybody with a good head and a good heart can "do it." Granted it may take a lifetime to learn to do it well, but there is no time like the present to get started. And from the first moment, it all seems to work out perfectly.

I am reminded of my time in South Africa during the period between Mandela's release and the All Races Election which marked the formal ending of Apartheid. Every moment was an adventure as the New South Africa was coming into being. Social institutions and practices were being tested and reinvented to serve the new reality with little experience to guide the process. Truthfully, nobody had ever quite been there before, and for sure the book had yet to be written. In one of the townships (South African designation for the Black areas), by the name of Tembesa, a major focus was economic development. Several hundred people had shown up for an Open Space, all of whom cared very deeply about the future of that town. Issues, ideas, plans and proposals flew in abundance for several days, and by the end it seemed that people had made a good start towards finding Peace for themselves, and enhanced economic productivity. By the time I got to bed it was very late, and I was totally bushed, so when my phone rang at 6:00 the next morning, I was anything but pleased or clearheaded. My confusion was compounded when the party at the other end sang out, "It worked! It worked! It worked!" When I had gathered my wits sufficiently to speak, I said as politely as I could, "Who are you, where are you, and what worked?"

It turned out that my caller had been a participant in Tembesa. He was also the president of what we in the United States would call a Parent/Teachers Association. For several years he had tried everything he could think of to energize the parents to take some proactive role in the education of their children, and nothing seemed to do any good. When he left the gathering at Tembesa, he went straight to yet another meeting of the PTA. Feeling he had nothing to lose, he tried a little Open Space, which as he ecstatically informed me, WORKED! Significantly he had read none of my books (which weren't written at the time), nor had he been to any training programs. He just did it.

The Practice of Peace, as I have come to understand it, is a purely natural act, rather like breathing and walking. Most of us, fortunately, come reasonably well equipped for both activities, and under normal circumstances, give little thought to either. That said, it is also true that an enormous distance separates the majority of us mortals from world class athletes. For the Olympians, breathing and walking (running) are raised to a whole new level. And the means of elevation is *practice.*

The word, practice, is a rich one indeed. In the world of athletics, practice commonly refers to the repetitive performance of key activities, be that specific plays for the game, or motions critical to clearing a hurdle or circling the track. In some sports this is known as "Doing the Reps," endlessly, but not mindlessly. There is an analytical element to practice, as the present activity is critiqued in the search for improvement. The physics, chemistry, to say nothing of the physiology involved are scrutinized for any possible advantage. Most people can run, but only the very few can regularly run a four-minute mile. For superb performance, natural gifts must be combined with superior technique, which brings us to the second level of meaning for the word *practice:* a professional skill. But most people know, certainly all athletes, that superior natural gifts and outstanding professional skills do not an Olympian make.

The difference between an individual possessing great natural gifts combined with outstanding professional skills, and a truly great athlete, is something more than simply the addition of greater gifts and skills. This "plus" is often referred to as *focus,* the ability to bring all natural gifts and learned skills to bear in the present moment to the exclusion of any possible distractions. My preferred word would be *presence.*

Presence, for me, is more than the capacity to focus on the details and broad scene, there is also an integrative quality which allows for the inclusion and blending of all natural gifts and learned skills. More than anything else, presence is not so much an action, but a quality of being which manifests itself both in action and stillness. We all have presence, but some of us have massive presence. And each of us can increase our presence with practice.

Phil Jackson, coach of the Los Angeles Lakers, and previously the Chicago Bulls, is arguably one of the great coaches of all times, not only in terms of the number of titles he and his teams have won, but also in terms of his demonstrated ability to take players of great gifts and skills and weld them into a team. Needless to say, many people, obviously including the opposing coaches, are more than a little curious as to how he does it, not just once, but year after year. If you listen to Phil, it is all about practice, certainly in the two senses mentioned previously, but also in a third sense: Practice as a Spiritual

Discipline. I am not sure that he would be totally comfortable with use of such words publicly, but in fact I have heard him say just that. And his players confirm that Phil Jackson is known to invite the group to meditate together.

I am in no position to judge the relative merits of Phil Jackson's approach to coaching, nor would I be willing to suggest that meditation is the only way to go. But when it comes to our preparation for the Practice of Peace, I believe it to be critical to understand Practice at all three levels. We need to do our "reps," everyday, for Peacemaking is an everyday task and opportunity. We will find that the need is omnipresent, and for sure we will get better with repetition. We also must build the skills and knowledge, for as our world changes and continues to change, old approaches will be seen in new ways, and new ways to Peace will show themselves. And last, but by no means least, there is the Spiritual Discipline. Putting ourselves on the line as Peacemakers without presence and focus will mean that we will be less than effective. And from a personal point of view, we will discover, to our pain, that the demands of the moment are more than sufficient to fry our Spirit, unless that Spirit is constantly restored.

DOING OUR "REPS"

There is an old cliché to the effect that *Peace begins at home.* Like many clichés that have the well worn feeling of pebbles in a brook, the truth may be obvious, but it is also profound. Every moment of every day, and in every situation, the forces of chaos, confusion and conflict do their natural work, opening space for new opportunities to appear, overwhelming previously convinced minds so that they can embrace new thoughts, and sharpening half-baked ideas and approaches into well-formed tools. Absent chaos, confusion and conflict, life stops. But if the toxic byproducts of discord, fragmentation and dis-ease are not constantly dealt with, they soon reach a lethal level, particularly if the physical, emotional, intellectual and spiritual space becomes limited, or closed. When we run out of space, the toxins are concentrated, and will overwhelm. Waiting until disaster strikes is not a good idea, for at that moment life quite literally hangs by a thread.

The daily work of Peace must be done clear across the board, at all levels and all quadrants of our existence (Ken Wilber). In our personal relationships with colleagues, friends and families, we need to remember Myrna Deckert's admonition, *Keep the Space Open.* When it comes to major projects, be that a new business, or public programs for education, nutrition or economic development, we need lots of space so that the complex adaptive system that we are has the room to grow and evolve, utilizing all the talents of everyone who cares.

How we do all this is a choice to be made in the moment, adopting an approach appropriate to that moment. Open Space Technology will certainly work in many situations, but more usually the Open Space Mentality will do better. But no matter the means or the setting, every time we have the privilege of opening space, we become better at it. While it is seemingly true that it always works, and anybody can do it, practice does help. We need to do the "reps."

BUILD THE KNOWLEDGE AND SKILLS

The Practice of Peace, like any other practice, requires a strong base of knowledge and skills. Basic research into the function of self-organizing systems proceeds in ever widening circles. Something that didn't even have a name forty years ago, or at least a name that anybody would recognize, now comes close to being a new academic discipline with a unique vocabulary, and captivating discoveries. What may save this new enterprise from the slow death of academic isolation is that the phenomenon of self-organization seems to cross all known fields. Nobody owns it, and everybody can benefit from the newest discoveries.

If basic research opens up new vistas, they are vistas without functions, and remain so until the fundamental insights are put to work in practical applications. The world of high technology has put the powers of self-organization to work to assist with some of the heavy lifting of computer systems development, essentially encouraging the system to grow itself.[34] Open Space Technology has provided similar opportunities in the area of human systems, many new applications are appearing almost daily.

If the procedure is set, and the general results predictable, the specifics of each application are surprising, and therefore create the opportunity for deeper understanding, both of the method and the systems worked with. The engagement in Rome was, from beginning to end, a powerful and often painful learning experience, even though as an Open Space, it was by no means remarkable. My learning included such things as the remarkable resilience of the human spirit in the face of incredible obstacles. I knew we as a species could handle a lot, but in the presence of that remarkable group of people, the bar was raised significantly. Given the condition of our world, this was good news indeed.

The areas for possible new developments are as various as the many facets of the human endeavor. One such area, which

---

[34] See Kevin Kelly's book, *Out of Control,* Addison-Wesley Publishing Co., 1994.

has always intrigued me, and where some significant work has been done, is that of education at all levels. It has been some years since I have had any close and sustained contact with school systems, but when I did, I often felt that entering a school was not unlike entering a war zone. Students appeared to be at war with themselves and each other, aligned only against the faculty, which in turn conflicted with the administration. Parents and other onlookers kept their distance, but should they let down their guard, they too joined the battle. If schools are supposed to be the nurturing places for our young, one might wonder what our young are being nurtured for. Question: What would happen if you opened space in a school? Several colleagues have done just that, and the results have been both predictable and remarkable. Predictable, in that the Open Space worked just fine, which is just another way of saying that schools and school people are complex adaptive systems like everything else. What was remarkable was that deeply conflicted parties (students, teachers, administration and parents) found it quite possible to talk usefully with each other. Perhaps most interesting was that students took to Open Space like ducks to water. Any thought that these young people would not be able to match their passion with responsibility was just plain wrong. So called "behavior problems" virtually disappeared, and learning at all levels took place with alacrity.

Should you ask me to supply the numbers that would prove my rosy assertions, I have to confess that we do not have too many. Conducting rigorous studies and publishing the results has not been a major concern with those who have employed Open Space around the world. Almost to a person such people have been "doers" and not academics. Anecdotal evidence exists in abundance, in print and online,[35] but rigorous studies are few and far between. I see this as a wonderful opportunity for those inclined to do such studies. The inhabitants of what many refer to as The Open Space Community are remarkably open, and more than willing to share their experience. It remains only to document and quantify what has happened to date. Or better yet, replicate the experiment (do an Open Space), with all necessary pre- and post-tests.

In sum, the knowledge and skill base for The Practice of Peace is more than rudimentary, but far from fully developed. This situation represents major opportunities in all directions. For those interested in building their own skill base, there is more than sufficient opportunity to get started. And for those interested in charting new territory, believe me, it is all open space.

THE PRACTICE OF PEACE AS A SPIRITUAL DISCIPLINE

The presence or absence of Peace impacts all aspects of our lives, economic, social, governmental, corporate, family—but, so far as I am concerned, Peace is fundamentally a matter of the Spirit. Spirit is one of those words, like Peace and Love, which has been subjected to an almost endless set of meanings. Indeed, for some people, it is a word without meaning. This situation seems to exist primarily in the West, or western influenced parts of the world, where the acids of scientific rationalism, by whatever name, have unfortunately (I believe) stripped away anything that cannot be seen, touched, tasted and ultimately counted and controlled. Getting a number on

---

[35] Perhaps the best source for such material is the archives of the Open Space Community Listserve: OSLIST@LISTSERV.BOISESTATE.EDU which you may access by visiting http//listserv.boisestate.edu/archives/oslist.html. You may also wish to visit www.openspaceworld.com and www.openspaceworld.org.

something somehow makes it real. And anything without a number is consigned to the realm of phantasm. Most of the rest of the world perceives Spirit in a rather different way, and even in the cathedrals of Science, the presence of Spirit is not unknown, or unacknowledged. During my tenure at the National Institutes of Health, where discourses on Spirit were hardly encouraged, it seemed that Spirit persisted in showing up in those special moments when eminent scientists conferred (usually privately) about the heart and soul of their work. Great work was described as *inspired*—which means literally in-spirited. And the *Spirit of Scientific Inquiry* was the seeming touchstone for the most important decisions. When it was present, good science was done. And in its absence no amount of hard work could justify the results.

I have no interest in entering into the debate, or offering some new definition of Spirit which might satisfy the skeptics. In fact, Spirit for me is one of those things that simply defies definition, and at some significant level, requires no definition. We know it when we meet. When world class athletes compete, we may be impressed with the technique and physical endurance, but the victory always seems to go to that individual or team with "Spirit." In the tormented, war-torn corners of our planet, the physical destruction may be immense, but the full reality of the situation hits us in the wane smiles of orphaned children whose Spirit shows through despite the absence of trust, respect and hope. In the waning moments of a failed business, as employees file out the door for the last time, it does not require esoteric skills to perceive that The Spirit of the place is snake belly low. In a word, we know Spirit when we meet.

The ultimate goal of The Practice of Peace, so far as I am concerned, is healing the Human Spirit. That done, and everything else seems to pretty well take care of itself. Of course, potholes remain in the roads and the economic infrastructure may be in total disarray, but when the Human Spirit finds it possible to re-assemble itself, such difficulties can usually be dealt with. In my experience, the special agent of healing (at least from the outside) is the Silent Witness of the Peacemaker standing as a solid rock in shifting sand or a strong tree in a high wind, offering a point of reference and support. A shattered Spirit is its own best healer, provided it has some place to start, and a little something to hold on to as the journey begins, a journey which in chaotic times is none other than the journey of Griefwork itself. Through shock, anger, denial, memories, and the silence of open space, the enduring presence of the Silent Witness follows the path, not to make it easier, wipe away the pain, or short circuit the trip, but to add the strength of a good companion.

Following that path in the company of those who travel it is perhaps the highest calling that any of us may hear, and it is surely one of the most demanding. Which brings into focus a second sense in which the Practice of Peace is a Spiritual Discipline, not practiced for others, but for ourselves.

Speaking strictly from personal experience, I can say with no qualification that in those instances when I have been privileged to accompany the likes of the 50 Palestinians and Israelis gathered in Rome, I have felt my personhood fulfilled as in no other way. I can also say with the same absoluteness, that no other experience in my life demanded so much. I knew that everything I had was on the line, and that line was a constantly moving target, requiring more, and more, and more, until I had been drawn into areas of myself and my world previously unknown. The words fright and growth come to mind. I was certain I had reached my limits, and yet more was required. Putting it bluntly, I was afraid. And yet as I reached one limit, I experienced growth towards new ones, which in turn were surpassed by new demands. My sense of Now seemed almost infinite, and my Spirit simply flew. The Spiritual Discipline of the Practice of Peace did its work superbly.

I would believe that a similar experience awaits each person who undertakes The Practice of Peace. In retrospect it seems almost selfish, for the gifts I received were certainly equal to, and doubtless outweighed, anything I may have given. Such an experience is not to be entered into lightly, and like all similar experiences, if we actually knew what the demands and the costs would be prior to entry, we probably wouldn't go. But in hindsight the rewards so far exceed the costs as to be a total gift. I wish that gift for you.